Making a YOU Turn

An In-Depth Exploration Into Finding and Loving Yourself

Elaine Van Melle, PhD

 Daring to Share Global ™

Published by Elaine Van Melle
2024 ISBN: 9781069178107

Editor: Diana Reyers
Typeset: Greg Salisbury
Book Cover Design: Olli Vidal

DEDICATION

This Workbook is dedicated to anyone who has

a desire to change

and the courage to take the first step.

GRATITUDE

I am grateful to all my fellow travelers
whose experiences and insights helped shape this workbook.

There are too many of you to mention individually,
but you know who you are.

I thank each and every one of you from the bottom of my heart,

and

I look forward to continuing our journey together.

TESTIMONIALS

Having navigated many life choices and expecting more, I value Elaine's invitation and guidance in understanding my past, rediscovering myself, and preparing for future 'forks in the road.' Empowered by this knowledge, I'm motivated to chart a deliberate path forward, informed by self-awareness of who I want to be. In a busy world, finding time and clarity for this work is tough, but this workbook offers a pathway for self-discovery.

Cheryl Poth, PhD
Professor, University of Alberta
partner, mom, daughter, sister, aunt, friend, and colleague.

Elaine Van Melle touchingly recounts her painful journey through unlearning the beliefs and "normal" ways of being in a marriage within the twisted paths so many women were raised to follow. She invites us as active participants to join her on this journey inward. Elaine puts her well-honed intellect into the service of self-inquiry, helping us dive into our private problematic worlds. By so doing, she offers us a path to real change, real personal power, not only in our unique spheres but also beyond… As we now begin to ask ourselves what we can possibly do to help our ailing planet and how we can make a difference, she paves a road: by taking responsibility for who we are and how we show up, we begin transforming the only thing we really can change—ourselves. By making our U-turns and by becoming sensitive and present to our inner dilemmas we could contribute in an active way to changing our society's path forward.

Evelyn Sucher
Sister U-Turner

It's not surprising that Elaine Van Melle has created such a brilliant roadmap for those on the journey of self-discovery. This workbook represents the clarity and curiosity with which she lives her life. She has created a simple portal through which anyone looking to deepen their inner world and outer relationships can do so with the utmost compassion. Elaine makes the often messiness of being human seem far less daunting and way more liberating.

Hillary Larson

TESTIMONIALS

Feeling stuck and knowing something needs to change can be lonely and overwhelming, but not with Elaine as a companion and guide. In her warm and supportive voice, she brilliantly weaves personal experiences with expertly distilled information, clear, practical exercises, and meaningful reflections that make this book more than one to read, but one to "do" with your whole heart. I dare you to show up for the adventure Elaine lays out. And I celebrate the emergence of your wise, authentic, connected self at the end.

Tiffany Vara

This book may very well become a primary resource for my clientele. As a master trainer for more than three decades, one of my first endeavours with a new client is to identify their current barriers to health and wellness and create a plan to tackle them. Elaine engages the reader immediately by asking them to self-reflect with intention and then evaluate their current position and desire to change. Her honesty, logic, and systematic progression expertly walk the reader through their journey and truly creates a sense of support for a potentially scary task.

Tracie Smith-Beyak
Owner, Conquer Fitness Education
Global presenter, personal trainer, author & entrepreneur
canfitpro National Fitness Advisory Panel Alumni
conquerfitnesseducation.guru

As someone who has been on the path of moving from my head to my heart and body for guidance in life, I was immediately captivated by Making a YOU Turn. The workbook format is brilliant and uniquely engaging for the in-depth personal exploration that Elaine invites. Elaine's warmth, authenticity, and genius radiate from every page. Anyone participating in this treasure-filled workbook and process will benefit from Elaine's wide-ranging expertise as an education scientist, as well as her profound insights about the journey to true self-connection and self-fulfillment. If you are facing a major crossroads or turning point in your life, Making a YOU Turn will be an invaluable companion.

Vanessa Bradley Bocandé
Social Impact Investor, Self-Wisdom Coach

TABLE OF CONTENTS

Considering if this workbook is for you, what this workbook offers, and how to undertake your personal journey.

Exploring your dilemma, crossroad, and desire for change:

A Moment of Realization: My Journey Begins;
Guidepost 1 Describing your dilemma;
Guidepost 2 Recognizing you are at a crossroad;
Guidepost 3 Connecting to your Inner Wisdom;
Guidepost 4 Giving yourself permission to go on a journey.

Examining your driving forces and the road to self-connection:

How Did I Get So Lost? My Journey into the Past;
Guidepost 1 Examining your current level of self-connection;
Guidepost 2 Identifying your driving forces;
Guidepost 3 Considering your outer influences;
Guidepost 4 Re-examining your level of self-connection.

Finding your way home though self-acceptance:

Learning to Travel with Ease: My Journey Continues;
Guidepost 1 Tracking your progress;
Guidepost 2 Staying connected to your Inner Wisdom;
Guidepost 3 Deepening your journey;
Guidepost 4 Travelling with ease.

Inviting others on your journey:

The Importance of Sisterhood: Creating Community;
Guidepost 1 Exploring your circle of trust;
Guidepost 2 Asking open questions;
Guidepost 3 Learning to pause together;
Guidepost 4 Moving forward through silence.

FOREWORD

Surrounded by the people of the Sápara village of Llanchamacocha, I stood on the narrow dirt airstrip, getting ready to leave the alluring Amazon rainforest. I knew my path forward was forever changed by the profound and liberating experience I had immersed myself in over the previous twelve days.

In 2019, Elaine Van Melle and I, along with eight other women, journeyed deep into the rainforest in Ecuador as part of a six-month exploration of self, sisterhood, and truth. While there, we learned from each other, hiked in the teeming forest, and tapped into the ancient wisdom of indigenous partners and plants. As the founder of a thriving company, I chose this experience because I recognized that I had been riding a runaway rollercoaster of work and production for some time. I also realized that I had not been tuning in to what I needed amid the frenetic busyness of my everyday life. The trip was transformational for me as I became more attuned to my identity and true desires and, as a result, shifted the course of my life by moving from prioritizing work to savouring presence and pace.

Elaine played a critical role in my personal "you" turn and continues to be one of my most provocative and influential mentors.

Within the following pages of this self-directed, user-friendly, and practical guide, Elaine uses her sincere voice and accessible writing style to invite you to begin your "you" turn. Tapping into her expertise as an education scientist, Elaine explores and illustrates how our minds, bodies, and spirits unite in a cacophony of true knowing. As she takes the reader through the various stages of the "you" turn journey, she blends art and science with a fluidity that exudes her trademark quiet confidence and heart-centred insight.

Anchored in vulnerability, the workbook format of *Making a YOU Turn* invites reflection, experimentation, and playful ideation, which is analogous to how messy and imperfect it can be to recognize that you have arrived at a crossroad and have an opportunity to figure out which path to take. This workbook is unique because it relies on the reader's wisdom to take a non-linear approach to living into their experiences. It can be daunting being on the learning edge of exploring our consciousness to make a change. However, Elaine has created a vehicle that gives us the freedom to choose a variety of access points to expand self-awareness and deepen how connected we feel to ourselves.

Teri Riddle is the Founder and CEO of the Crossland Group, an equity-centered strategic advisory firm that sparks people's potential to care for themselves and enable thriving organizations for a more equitable world.

INTRODUCTION

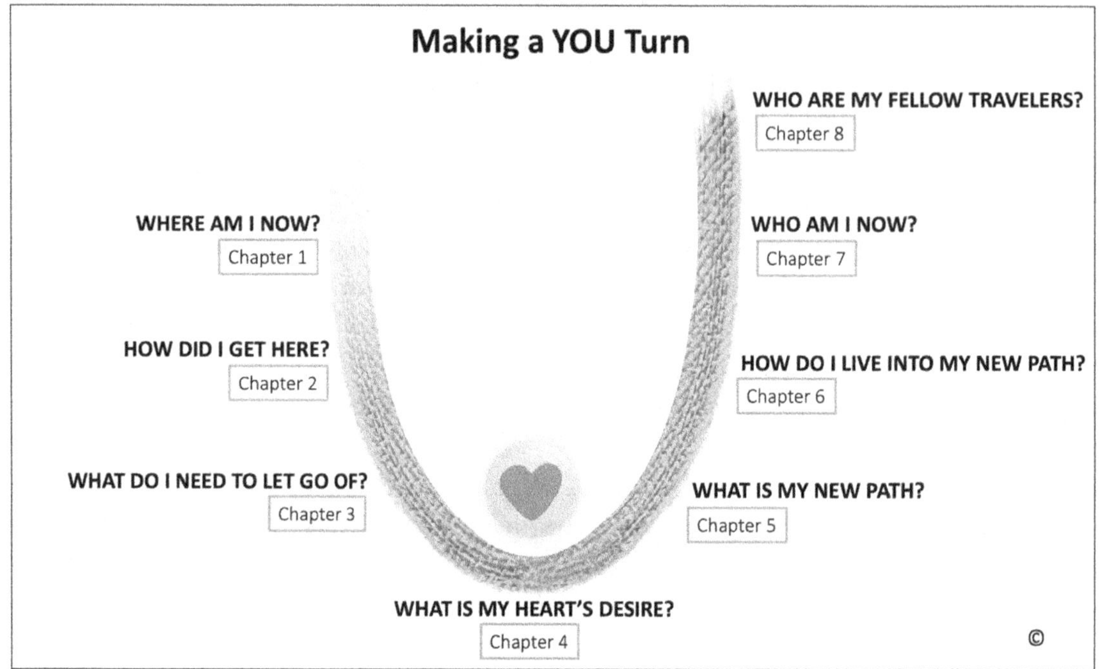

Are You Here?

Considering if this workbook is for you, what this workbook offers, and how to undertake your personal journey.

Odds are you've picked up this workbook, wondering if it is time to make a change.
You might be at a significant crossroads, feeling a bit lost, wondering which path to take.
Or perhaps you desire being fully present in your life
so that you and all you have to offer are firmly planted in the driver's seat.

You are in the right place if any of these words speak to you.

Helping you to connect to who you truly are, or what I like to refer to as
finding the essence of your presence is the central focus of this workbook.

This workbook follows the eight steps in the YOU Turn shown above.
The introduction provides an overview of what to expect and strategies for
making a successful YOU Turn.

Your journey begins here!

My journey began several years ago when I found myself questioning the direction of my marriage . *Should I stay or should I go?* This was the dilemma that fueled my first step. However, as I learned to carve my path, I discovered a more fundamental question to my journey.

How did I become so disconnected from my priorities and heart's desire?

I felt so very lost. Yet somehow, I knew I had to take full responsibility for reconnecting to my inner strength and wisdom. As an Education Scientist, I was well-versed in the literature describing transformative change. It was time to put my knowledge to work, so I sought out experts and participated in workshops that constantly challenged me to step out of my comfort zone. Being a voracious reader, I found books and articles that clearly spoke to why my life had become so driven by the needs and expectations of others. I gradually learned how to reconnect with my needs and unique gifts.

The eight steps of the YOU Turn capture my path toward living a fully connected life and provide the foundation for this workbook. Each chapter is carefully crafted, so you can take advantage of what I learned along the way. They are organized as follows:

- The chapter begins with an excerpt from my story illustrating the main theme;
- To begin your journey, you are invited to reflect on your connection to my story;
- What I learned along the way is then presented as four guideposts;
- Each guidepost is accompanied by an exercise designed to facilitate your journey;
- Each chapter ends with a description of key concepts and a list of references.

The details of your story and dilemma may very well differ from mine. However, the main themes and steps for making a YOU Turn are universal and will undoubtedly speak to you. I hope that sharing my story will pave the way for you to be honest with your story, allowing you to fully engage with the exercises.

The chapters are presented sequentially, with each step building on the last. However, the individual chapters and exercises can also stand alone. As you review the Table of Contents, if a specific theme or guidepost draws you in, feel free to start there. This workbook and process are designed as a self-directed journey and can unfold in any direction that works best for you.

You may desire to take this journey with others. If so, Chapter 8 will help you engage with your fellow travellers, and you may want to start there. However, as you begin your journey, you may find yourself traveling straight through the workbook. Or you may get started and find out life gets in the way. That's okay because you can always return to this workbook anytime. My intention is not to turn this into a *make-work project*, so I won't give you a *how-to recipe with a timeline*. Instead, here are some general suggestions to support your journey:

- Create or find a space that supports quiet reflection;
- Set aside a specific time during the day or week to undertake your travels;
- Consider attending retreats or workshops to support you along the way;
- Place this workbook in a spot that is readily accessible;
- Use the white space in the workbook to capture your experience.

The most successful strategy is to integrate the readings and exercises into your everyday routine—in whatever way feels right for you.

You may find that this work opens areas you have never explored. Please don't hesitate to find expert assistance if you ever feel overwhelmed or are having difficulty moving forward.

Although the YOU Turn illustration looks nice and neat, as you will come to know, I certainly encountered roadblocks and bumps along the way. However, throughout my YOU Turn I learned how to travel with ease, stay present, and make clear decisions even in the face of difficult situations. Today, as I continue going deeper and deeper into my YOU Turn, I remain fully in the driver's seat, no longer thrown off my path by forces out of my control—this is the transformation I was looking for.

As you travel through this workbook, I do not doubt you will experience whatever change you seek. It may take work and patience but always remember that you are well worth the journey.

I am beside you all the way.

Elaine Van Melle

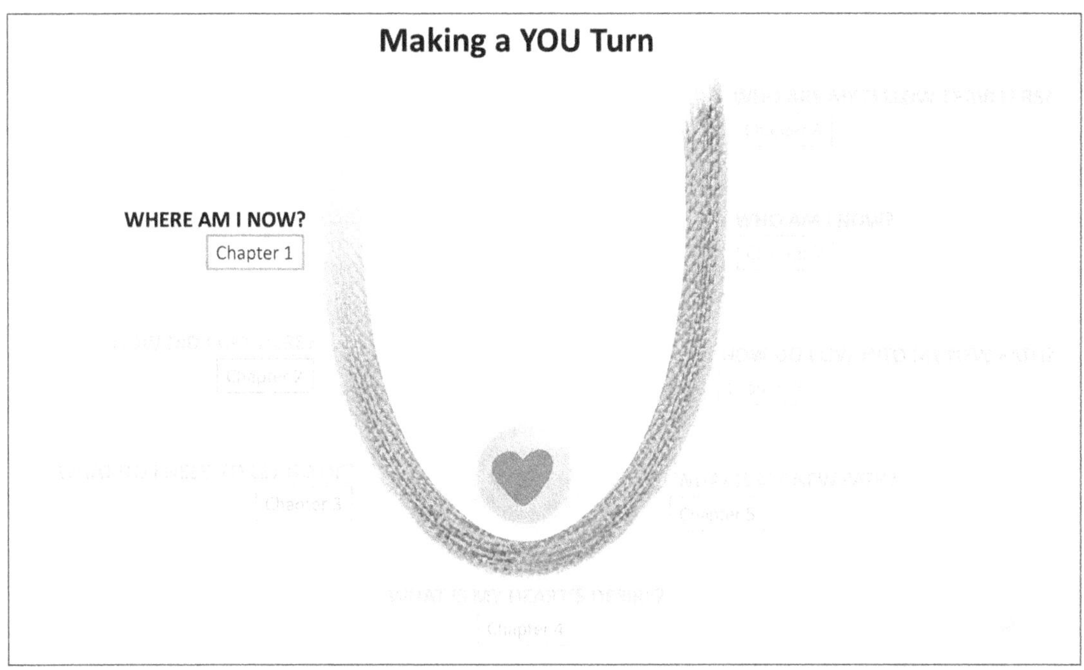

Chapter 1

Where Am I Now?

Exploring Your Dilemma, Crossroad, and Desire for Change

Every journey begins with a desire for change.
When undertaking a road trip, you will initially
look for a shift in your external environment—quite literally, a change in scenery.
However, a truly transformative journey begins when your inner landscape
calls for you to show up differently.

You may experience this invitation in the form of a whisper, a niggle, or an intuitive sense that
something is not quite as you would like it to be. Or, perhaps it doesn't present that softly but
instead more like a shout that you simply cannot ignore.

In this opening chapter you will have a chance to explore what brought
you here and your desire for change.

My Invitation to You

The story below captures my *Aha Moment.*
The moment I knew something had to change.

As you read about my experience, you will notice that my inner cues
presented as both a whisper and a shout.

As you read my story, please consider the following:

- Describe any connection you may have to my experience.

- Share any *moment of realization* or niggles or whispers that brought you to this workbook.

A Moment of Realization:
My Journey Begins

It is the summer of 2016. I am sitting on the couch at my cottage in the Laurentians, looking out through the wall of windows to a spectacular view. The weather is nothing short of perfect, but I am not taking it in. I am barely breathing as I sit hunched over, sad and withdrawn. In the kitchen, my partner of 29 years is starting his day and doing his thing, getting organized to go into town to begin fixing whatever needs to be fixed. This is now our routine. I do my thing, and he does his, and never the twain shall meet.

I long for intimacy—much more than the physical kind. Intimacy—in to me see—the kind where I am truly seen and valued for exactly who I am. It is when every muscle and cell in my body relaxes, I am held deeply safe, and I can melt into who I truly am. I long for this level of connection but am lost as to how to make this happen—how to break this lonely dance that has taken years to finesse.

A few weeks later, I share this sad story at our marriage therapy session. I thought I was telling a story of being held captive by his inattention, but underneath my story lies an unstated plea, "Please, please fix him so I can get what I need." The therapist challenges me and wonders why I chose to tell this story. At that moment, I wonder the same thing.

Sometimes, this happens as part of me seems to separate and hover over my body; it watches and listens with great curiosity. This observer part also asks, "What is keeping you on the couch? How did you get so lost?" At that moment, time stands still, and I lose all sense of place. My world narrows, and I become acutely aware of being in my body. A voice emerges from deep inside saying, "Perhaps it is you who needs to change."

This is how my journey begins.

Lessons Learned

The nature of your journey is so unique, complex, and unpredictable that you can only make sense of your individual experience in hindsight—as if looking in your rear-view mirror. For example, I could never have predicted that this particular moment at my cottage would prove to be so instrumental in starting me on a different path. After all, as I reveal in the following chapters, I had been navigating a difficult situation for many years. So, what was so special about this moment?

Ultimately and over time, I realized answering that question really isn't important. What matters are the following four guideposts:

1. Describing your dilemma;
2. Recognizing you are at a crossroad;
3. Connecting to your Inner Wisdom;
4. Giving yourself permission to go on a journey.

I expand on these guideposts and lessons learned below to support you as you start your own journey.

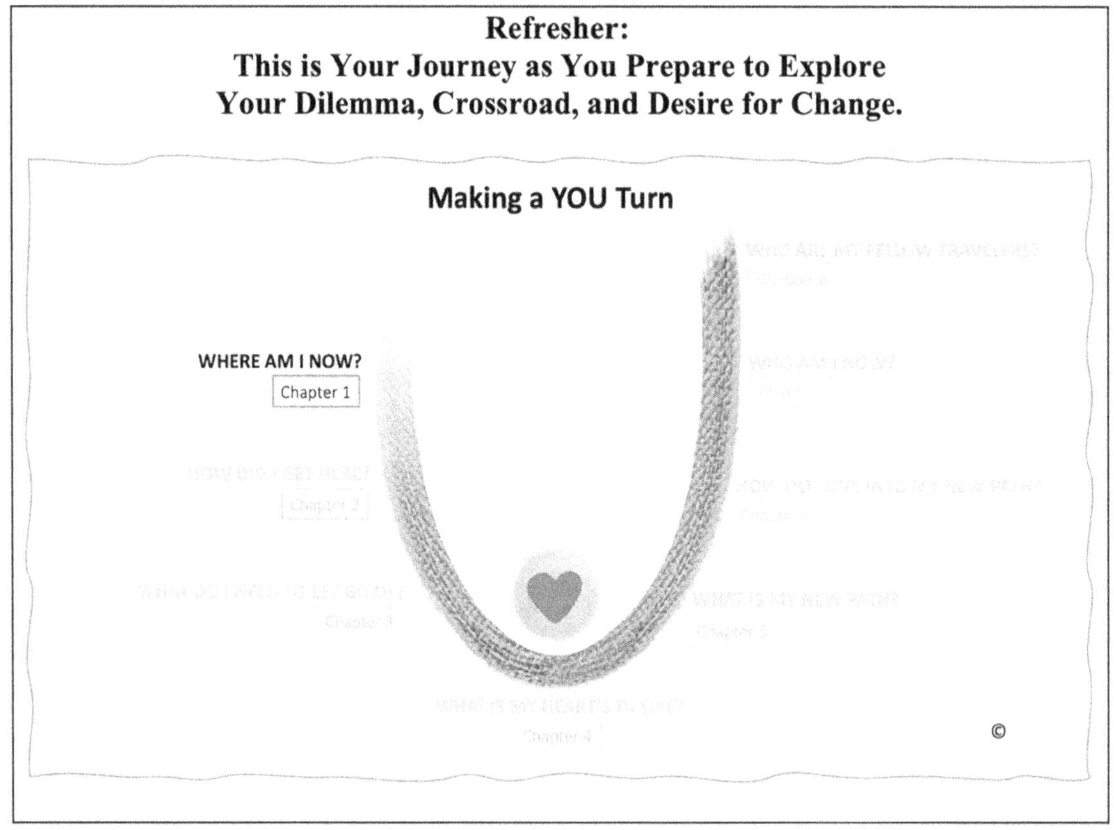

Guidepost 1: Describing your Dilemma

A desire to make a YOU Turn often starts with an unsettling experience or series of experiences that cause you to question your long-held beliefs and assumptions. For example, I must admit that throughout our marriage I probably believed the answer to any relationship problem lay in my husband's capacity to change or be fixed. You will come to learn that, given his increasing reliance on alcohol, it was not difficult to for me to be that self-righteous. However, as told in my story, this assumption was challenged by an inner whisper with the thought that perhaps I, rather than my partner, needed to change.

This thought was initially startling, yet I don't know why I was surprised because I believe that all common-change wisdom is based on the understanding that…

You cannot change someone else;
you can only change yourself.

Nonetheless, it took me some time to fully embrace my newfound understanding. I was so used to placing the blame for my discontent elsewhere and easily resisted the thought that I might need to do something differently. However, I became more excited the longer I thought about this possibility. It was very liberating to recognize that I had the freedom to choose a different path because I didn't need to rely on someone or something else to change. This became a significant shift for me. I felt as if I had crossed over a threshold and would never see or live in the world the same way again.

Embracing this shift allowed me to take responsibility and start my own YOU Turn.

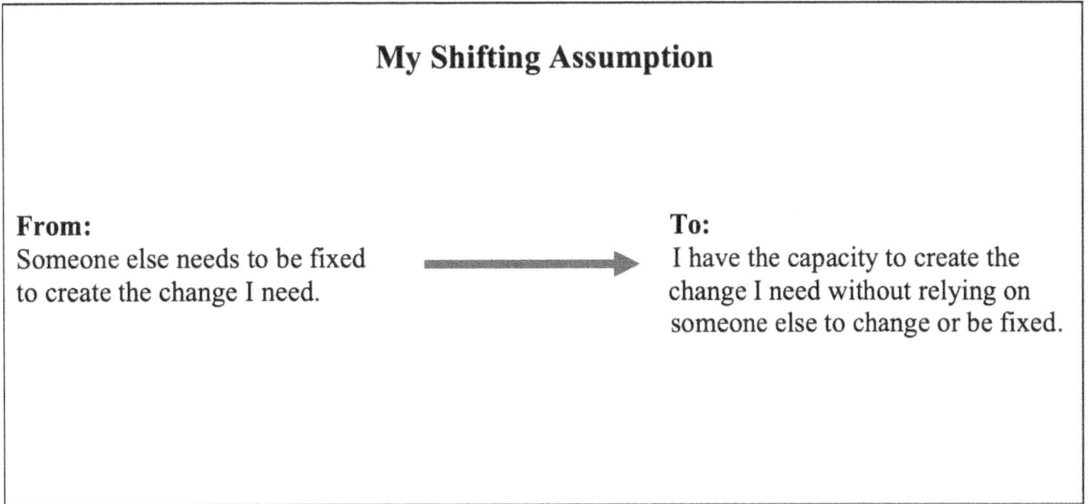

Now it's Your Turn

While reading my story, did you identify any moments of realization leading to your interest in making a YOU Turn? It could be any life experience. For example, a work or family relationship or a stage of life that is causing you to question if you are on the right path. As described in my example, these moments are unsettling because they cause you to question your long-held beliefs and assumptions. The purpose of this exercise is to give voice to the dilemma you are experiencing and capture what might be shifting for you.

As you complete this exercise, please keep in mind that assumptions and beliefs are often so entrenched that they exist well below the surface of your level of awareness. This makes it extremely challenging to unearth—to literally dig up—the beliefs that have been guiding you. So, take your time.

Feel free to revisit and revise your statements over the course of your journey. You will know you have arrived when the truth of your statement fully resonates with you. In that moment, you will begin to feel unstuck as new pathways begin to emerge.

Describing Your Dilemma

In the space below describe your dilemma. For example, you might be wondering:
- Why does my work no longer satisfy me as it used to?
- What is my role now that my children no longer need me?
- How can I move gracefully into the next stage of my life?

Now take some time to consider any assumptions and beliefs that might be shifting,
or need to shift, as you consider your dilemma.

From:　　　　　　　　　　　　　　　　　　　　　　　　　**To:**

Guidepost 2: Recognizing That You Are at a Crossroad

As illustrated in my story, my dilemma lay within my marriage. Simply stated, I came to the point where I was stuck and wondered, *Should I stay or go?* Clearly, my crossroad had serious life-changing implications. I had been married for 30 years. If I chose to leave, I wondered, *Would I have to leave my home of 21 years? Could I survive on my own? How could I let go of the life we built together for so long? What would the impact be on our children?* However, realizing that the time had come to make a choice was stabilizing. I had let myself be knocked off course by self-doubts, and the resulting confusion and uncertainty made it difficult to find any joy in life. It was also very freeing to realize that, at that moment, I was not committing to any specific decision. In fact, I did not know what lay ahead or what the outcome would be. Somehow, I knew this was just the beginning of my journey.

Now it's Your Turn

Not all turning points need to be as substantial as mine. Sometimes, smaller junctions are as important to acknowledge. Regardless of the implications, appreciating you are at a crossroad is a critical step. It allows you to acknowledge that, in facing your dilemma, you can choose to take a different path. This exercise is intended to be fairly straightforward. Keep in mind that this is for your eyes only, so be as honest as possible.

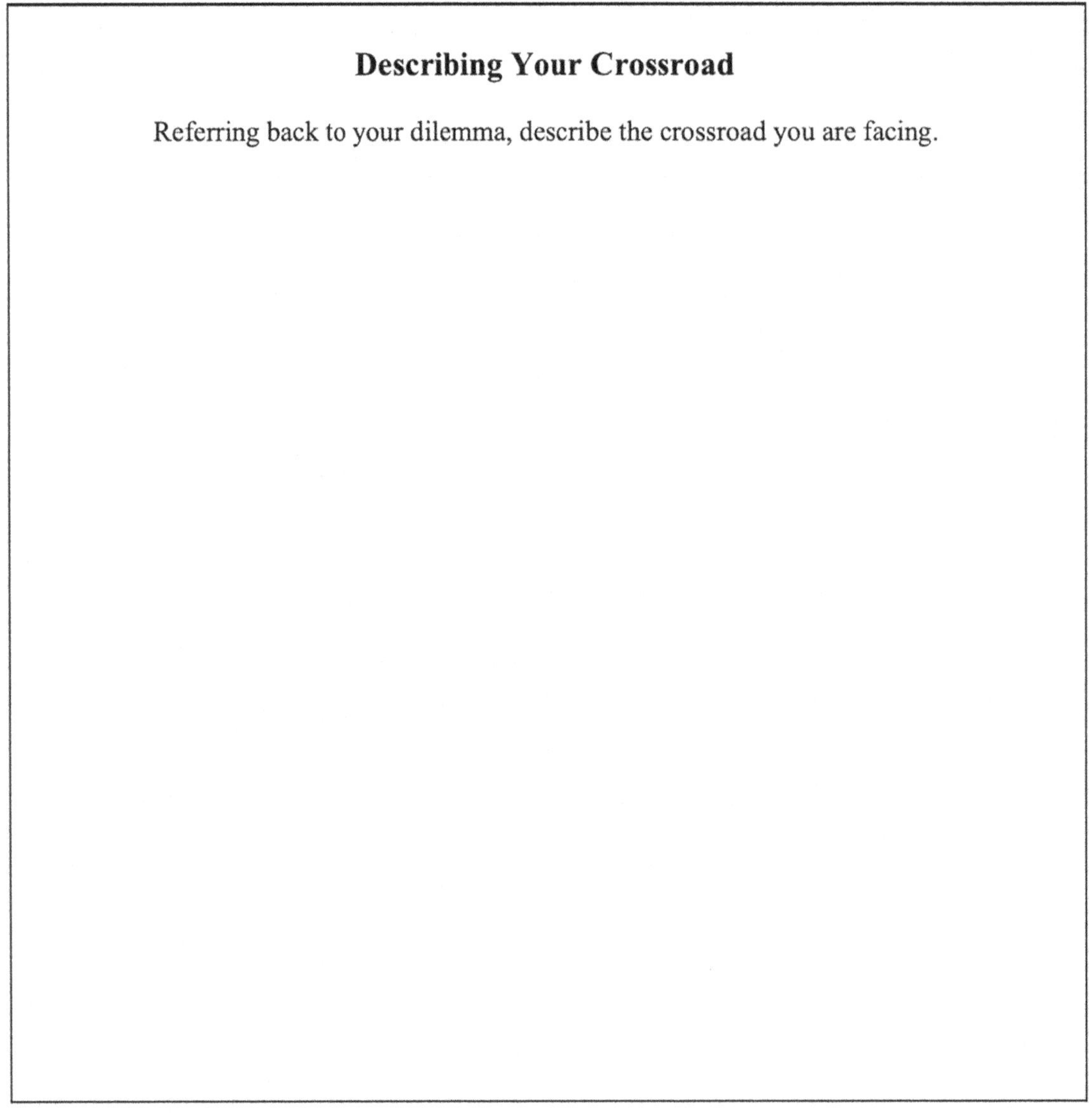

Guidepost 3: Connecting to Your Inner Wisdom

In my opening story, I describe becoming aware of a voice that seems to emerge spontaneously. I have always been somewhat aware of this presence, or what I now refer to as my *Inner Wisdom*. Over the course of my YOU Turn, I came to appreciate the importance of putting this voice firmly in the driver's seat. This required learning more about and strengthening this inner resource.

As I share with you my discoveries, I invite you to see if you can start to connect with your Inner Wisdom. However, it is important to remember that although we all have this voice, it often takes time and practice to get in touch with this part of you. In fact, this guidepost is just a starting point. Since connecting with your Inner Wisdom is such a critical step in making a YOU Turn, multiple opportunities are provided throughout this workbook to find your Inner Wisdom and strengthen your connection.

As a starting point, it may be helpful to know this Inner Wisdom can also be referred to as your:

- Inner Teacher;
- Voice;
- Authentic Self;
- True Self, or
- Soul.

to name a few. Feel free to choose a word or phrase that best captures your experience.

Following is what I learned while exploring my Inner Wisdom:

My Inner Wisdom . . .

- Is always with me;
- Embodies the core of who I am;
- Notices what I am thinking and feeling;
- Is non-judgmental;
- Has no agenda.

I also realized that my Inner Wisdom could be easily blocked out depending on the circumstances. For example, if I was really busy getting things done as well as drawn into difficult situations, louder, different voices could take over. When I was stuck, these voices often told me what I *should* be doing. However, over time, I recognized that my Inner Wisdom didn't operate from *shoulds*. As a result, I asked myself how to quiet these louder voices to let my Inner Wisdom shine through.

I reasoned that if this observing voice was always with me, there must be a way to access its wisdom, even in the most trying situations. So, I set out to see if I could strengthen my connection to my Inner Wisdom. I found that the following two strategies worked best for me.

Strategies for Connecting to my Inner Wisdom

- Develop an Image

I started imagining what I could look like when operating from my Inner Wisdom. As I took on its quality, I saw myself in flowy, white, soft, comfortable clothes. My face relaxed into a gentle smile, and my shoulders and arms easily hung by my side. To solidify this image, I created a visual collage which I labelled Wise Woman. In any situation, just visualizing this image helped me to access my Inner Wisdom.

- Find a Talisman

I have always been drawn to clear crystals, not so much for any potential healing or energy effects, but because I love the explosion of colour when the light hits the crystal just the right way. This rainbow effect represents an opening of multiple possibilities in the same way that listening to my Inner Wisdom can reveal new pathways. As a result, I adopted a clear crystal as a tangible talisman, representing the feeling of operating from my Inner Wisdom.

What I love about these two strategies is that, regardless of what I'm doing, even when I'm in the middle of a storm, I can simply take a breath, recall the image of my Wise Woman or the light hitting my crystal and begin to tap into the voice of my Inner Wisdom. Over time, the experience became very physical—connecting with my Inner Wisdom was accompanied by feeling completely at home in my body. I felt acutely aware of all my emotional and physical sensations. I literally felt myself moving out of my head as I shifted from doing into being. I completely understood that, when my Inner Wisdom was present, I experienced a great sense of:

- Calm, where any inner turmoil I was experiencing completely stilled;
- Clarity, where I could easily see my next steps and
- Curiosity, where I was genuinely inquisitive about what was happening with myself and others.

Overall, I shifted from being in a reactive state to being much more open and grounded. For example, as I describe in my story when I become aware of my Inner Wisdom, I lose all sense of my surroundings and am completely in tune with my physical presence. My vision turns inward as my body fully relaxes into the moment. I lose all tension in my facial muscles and shoulders. I am naturally still, and a calmness descends over me. My curiosity becomes piqued as I tap into my Inner Wisdom. I listen without judgement, and I feel fully alive.

Again, connecting with your Inner Wisdom takes time and practice. The following exercise is designed to help you get started.

Now it's Your Turn

Each of us has an inner knowing; an intuitive sense that guides us from deep within. Given the busyness of our day-to-day lives and the level of noise that often surrounds us, it is easy to tune-out or ignore this Inner Wisdom. The purpose of this exercise is for you to begin to tune into your own sense of inner knowing. Connecting to this Inner Wisdom is critical to making a You Turn. But be patient with yourself. You have the whole workbook to find and strengthen this connection.

Connecting to Your Inner Wisdom

- Reflect on how easy or hard is it to connect to your own Inner Wisdom?

- Describe a time when your Inner Wisdom was present: where were you and what were you doing?

- Share any physical sensations and feelings that were part of your experience.

- What strategies could you use to strengthen your connection to your Inner Wisdom?

Guidepost 4: Giving Yourself Permission to Undertake Your Journey

As part of Chapter 1, you described one of your crossroads: the dilemma you are facing. You understand the importance of finding and drawing from your Inner Wisdom to stay the course. Now what?

At one point, when I was feeling really lost early on, one of my journal entries read:

> *Find yourself; it's been too long.*
> *Trust yourself; it will make you strong.*

These simple words became my mantra—my way of giving myself permission to focus on myself through my journey. Why was this permission so important?

Too often, many equate spending time on themselves as being selfish. You may ask yourself, *How can I be considerate of others if I am solely focused on my needs?* This is a particularly important question in this day and age with so many global challenges and suffering going on around you.

In response, it is essential to recognize that this journey does not need to be all-encompassing. As described in the introduction, you can readily balance these exercises with other priorities in your life. However, I promise you that as you rediscover yourself, making a YOU Turn will no longer feel like an exercise but simply how you show up.

This is when who you truly are becomes the essence of your presence.

I think of living this way as being *self-full*. Ultimately, your capacity to be self-full will fuel your ability to be there for others. Consequently, permitting yourself to embark on this journey of self-discovery is the most powerful gift you can give to yourself as well as those who rely on you.

Now it's Your Turn

At this point in your journey, you have a sense that something needs to change. The details will emerge as you go through the workbook but for now you are engaging because something inside of you is saying it is time. Your mantra is a phrase that speaks directly to this desire. It is a phrase that when repeated reminds you of why you are making a YOU Turn.

Giving Yourself Permission to Go On a Journey:
Creating Your Mantra

Create a saying or a mantra that captures your motivation for going on this journey.

In Summary

Chapter 1 focused on taking the time to acknowledge your current situation. Perhaps getting to this point has been a long time coming. You may experience a great deal of clarity and relief in getting started. Or you may be just getting started on connecting to your Inner Wisdom and have yet to land on describing your crossroad. It doesn't matter. What matters is that you have bravely taken the first steps towards putting yourself firmly in the driver's seat. In the following chapters, you will learn how to create a solid connection with your Inner Wisdom and make your mantra come to life as you continue on your YOU Turn.

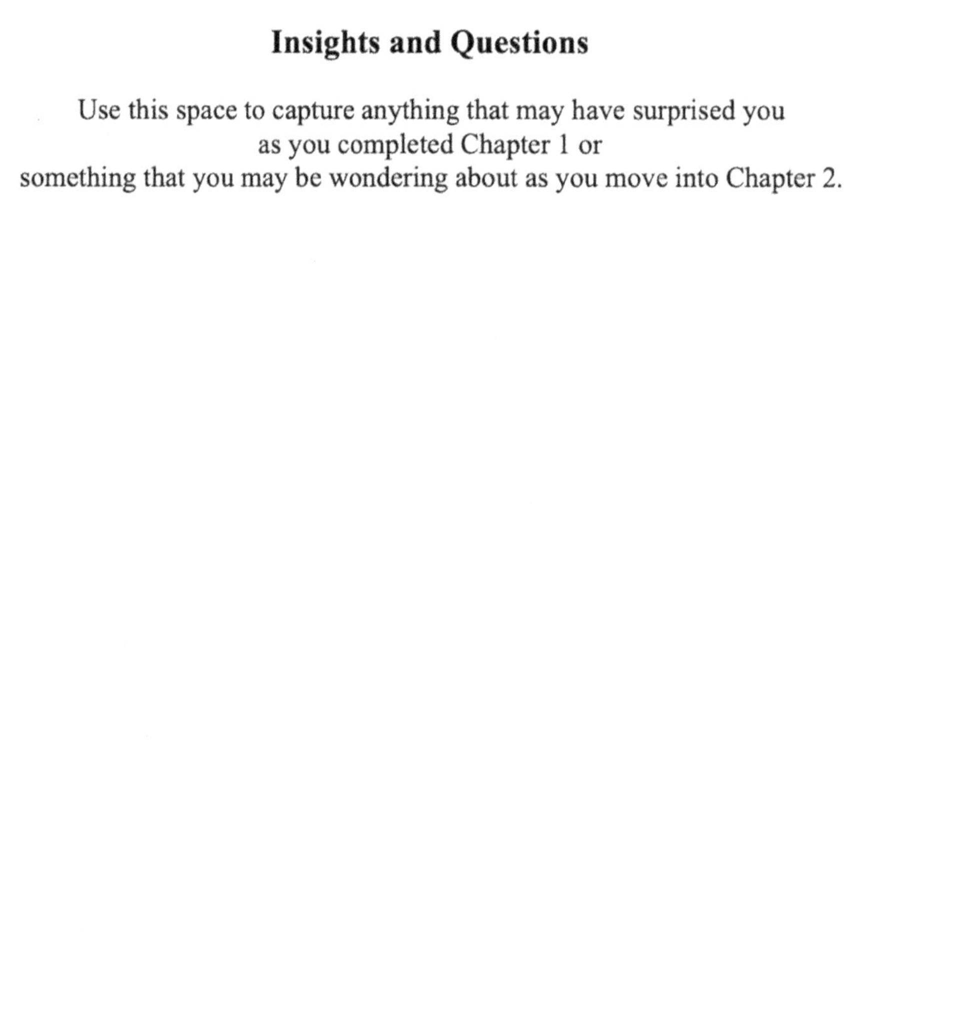

Insights and Questions

Use this space to capture anything that may have surprised you
as you completed Chapter 1 or
something that you may be wondering about as you move into Chapter 2.

Key Concepts

Crossroad or Dilemma
An internal and personal crisis where it is recognized that previous beliefs, approaches, and solutions are no longer adequate. (see Mezirow, 2000, p. 298.)

Inner Wisdom
An inner voice that you can trust to guide you in the right direction.

Mantra
A short statement, phrase or word that captures the reason for your journey, and when repeated, provides support for continuing your YOU Turn.

Transformative Change
The process by which we shift out of our taken-for-granted frames of references (meaning perspectives, habits of mind, mind-sets) to make them more inclusive, discriminating, open, emotionally capable of change and reflective so that they may generate beliefs and opinions that will prove more true or justified to guide how we act and behave. (see Mezirow, 2000: p.7-8.)

The Transformative Process
Transformation can be brought about by:
- a single major event leading to a shift in beliefs,
- a series of cumulative events leading to a shift in beliefs,
- a deliberate conscious effort to examine and change one's beliefs, and/or
- the developmental progression of becoming more mature. (see Cranton, 2006, p. 57)

References

Conner J. (2008). Writing Down Your Soul. How to Activate and Listen to the Extraordinary Voice Within. San Francisco, CA: Conari Press.

Cranton P. (2006). Understanding and Promoting Transformative Learning. Second edition. San Francisco, CA: Jossey-Bass.

Mezirow J. (2000). Learning as Transformation: Critical Perspectives on a Theory in Progress. San Francisco, CA: Jossey-Bass.

Palmer P.J. (2004). A Hidden Wholeness: The Journey Toward an Undivided Life. San Francisco, CA: Jossey-Bass.

Prendergast J.J. (2015). In Touch. How to Tune In to the Inner Guidance of Your Body and Trust Yourself. Boulder, CO: Sounds True, Inc.

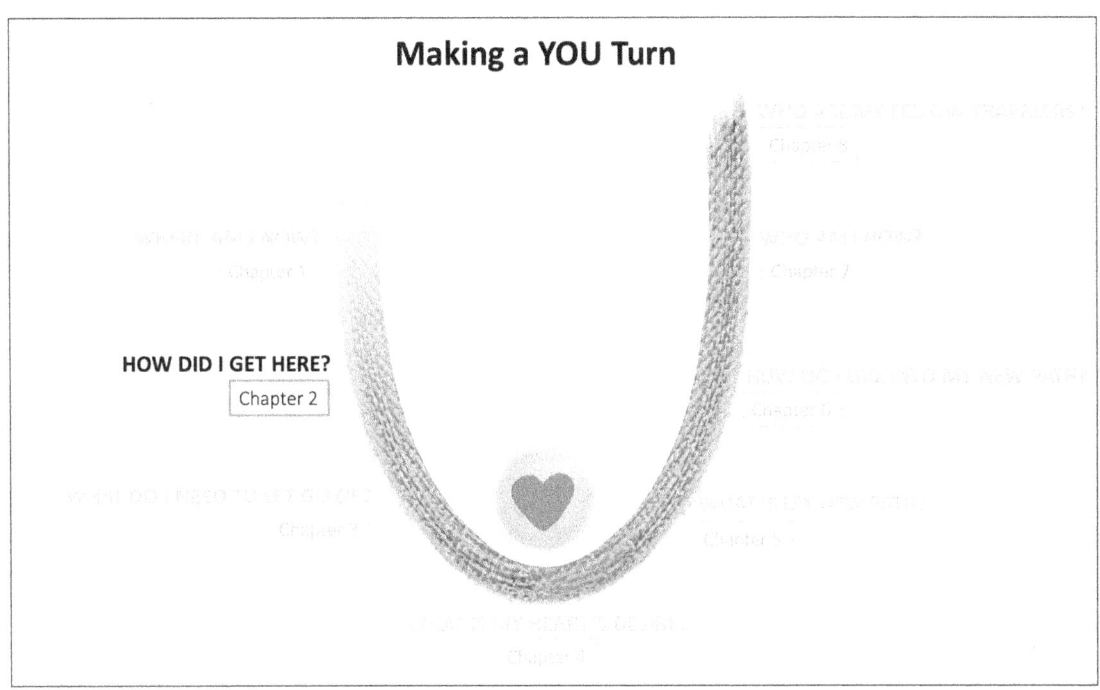

Chapter 2

How Did I Get Here?

Examining Your Driving Forces and the Road to Self-Connection

In Chapter 1, you clarified your dilemma, the issue that fuels your desire for change. Dilemmas often require making difficult choices. At this point in your journey, the way forward is probably not very clear. However, as introduced in Chapter 1, the main premise of this workbook is that clarity comes when you create a strong connection to your Inner Wisdom.

This is what it means to make a YOU Turn.

In Chapter 2, you will use *The Continuum of Self-Connection* to focus on examining your level of self-connection. This includes considering the role of your background experiences and how the world we live in tends to encourage disconnecting from your Inner Wisdom.

A word of warning—fasten your seatbelt because it's going to be a bumpy ride!!

18

My Invitation to You

The story below describes an experience that describes how lost I felt.
As you read my story, consider the following:

- What words best describe how you feel when you think of your current situation? For example, I feel confused, lost, off-course, adrift, bewildered, to name a few.

- Recall a moment that best reflects your feeling.

How did I Get So Lost?
My Journey into the Past

It is the spring of 2015. My partner and I are at a marriage workshop in Toronto run by Dr. Terry Real, a psychologist specializing in marriages on the brink. A few years ago, I read his book "I Don't Want to Talk About It" in which he explores the phenomenon of male depression. Every word resonated with me.

Given that my husband was clearly drinking, I wondered if this was the right route. I talked to Dr. Real, and he reassured me, "Yes, I have a lot of experience with addictions. You should come."

The workshop is being held in a large room on the university campus. The two of us sit side-by-side with Terry and five other couples in a circle in the centre of the room. We are surrounded by a ring of therapists positioned at a distance, sitting against the walls of the room. They have come to observe and learn. The idea of showing my vulnerability in front of all these therapists is overwhelming—it's hard to stay present. But I'm desperate to find a way forward and trust Terry's expertise.

He calls the couples into the spotlight one by one. We are the third couple invited. I sit on one side of Terry, and my partner sits on the other. I look at him. He seems so shrunken and defeated, and yet, despite not wanting to be here, he has shown up, knowing how important this is to me. I feel a surge of love combined with great sadness. I question, "How in the world did we get here?"

I am so nervous that the session seems to go by in a blur, except when Terry asks me a question, and I provide a sudden, startling response. I feel a jolt deep in my gut and gaze towards my partner. I was inexplicably drawn to him at that moment despite all that had happened. Time stands still, and everything in the room fades. An invisible force creates a connection to him, and I experience a deep knowing that, somehow, this energy has kept me in my unhealthy situation for so long. As he watches my reaction, Terry states, "You have codependence written all over your face." I feel diagnosed and labelled as I look down at my feet and shrink into my chair, wanting to disappear. My inner wisdom is strangely silent, and I am totally confused about how to move forward.

At this point, I feel completely lost.

Lessons Learned

The details of your story may be very different from my vignette presented above. However, I don't doubt that your degree of vulnerability required to recall a similar moment may be the same as mine. In fact, reading this part of my story eight years after experiencing it, I felt so raw and exposed that I hesitated to include it in this workbook. And because I am now so far past this point of feeling so lost and disconnected, I wondered—*Do I really need to go there?*

Ultimately, I left it in because pretending this journey is not without challenges would lead you down a garden path. To commit to being fully vulnerable is a necessary part of making a YOU Turn. I also recognized that, for your journey, it is essential that you are honest with yourself only. It is entirely up to you how much of your story you wish to share with others.

At this point in our journey, the following 4 guideposts are most important:

1. Exploring your level of self-connection;
2. Identifying your driving forces;
3. Considering your outer influences;
4. Revisiting your level of self-connection.

Refresher:
Tapping into Your Inner Wisdom

Use a strategy from Guidepost 3 in Chapter 1
and take a minute to connect to your Inner Wisdom.

Your Inner Wisdom will be a helpful companion as you travel through Chapter 2.

Write a few words below about this experience: describing the level of ease or discomfort with which you connected to your Inner Wisdom and whether you experienced any sensations, sounds, or images that confirm you made the connection.

Guidepost 1: Exploring Your Level of Self-Connection

As I describe in my story, I was incredibly uncomfortable being labelled *codependent* But when an accomplished therapist whose work I had come to admire and trust tells me something, I listen. So, I went into my natural researcher mode.

I learned that the term codependent was originally described in relation to *people whose lives had become unmanageable as a result of living in a committed relationship with an alcoholic* (Beattie, 1992, p. 34). I could certainly check that box. Further research revealed lists and lists of behaviours of the codependent person. It was all a bit overwhelming and many behaviours did not resonate with me. To be honest, despite researching codependence and engaging in numerous Al-Anon meetings, I ended up more lost and confused.

As I continued my journey, I came across a PhD thesis on codependency, which helped me turn a significant corner. Instead of working from a list of predefined behaviours or labels, this researcher explored the lived experience of codependency from the perspective of self-identified codependents (Bacon, 2015). I devoured every word.

Interestingly, codependency was not just equated with being in a relationship with an alcoholic but was described as contributing to a wide range of life difficulties. The pieces fell into place when I finally came across the following phrase describing the common experience of the participants:

> *All shared the experience of struggling
> to locate and define a clear sense of self.*

As I read this statement, I realized I didn't really have a clue as to who I was or what I needed. No wonder my Inner Wisdom was so silent. I found myself moving past the question of whether codependency was the correct label for me and instead appreciated the more important point that:

> *Somewhere along the way, I lost connection to myself,
> making me vulnerable to placing priority on others' needs
> rather than mine.*

Continuing in my researcher mode, I reasoned that I knew very well what it felt like to be *disconnected*. However, to move forward, I had to be equally clear about what it looked like to be self-connected. This line of exploration led me to create *The Continuum of Self-Connection*.

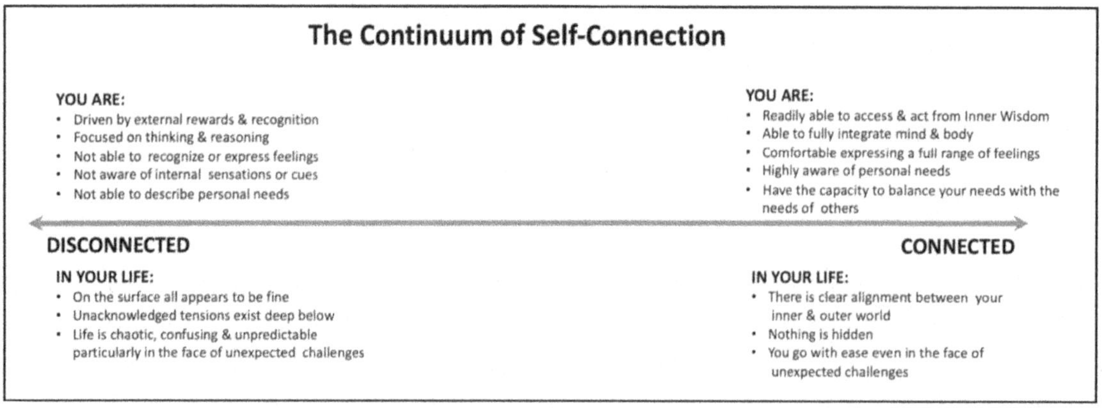

The Continuum of Self-Connection

YOU ARE:
- Driven by external rewards & recognition
- Focused on thinking & reasoning
- Not able to recognize or express feelings
- Not aware of internal sensations or cues
- Not able to describe personal needs

YOU ARE:
- Readily able to access & act from Inner Wisdom
- Able to fully integrate mind & body
- Comfortable expressing a full range of feelings
- Highly aware of personal needs
- Have the capacity to balance your needs with the needs of others

DISCONNECTED ⟷ **CONNECTED**

IN YOUR LIFE:
- On the surface all appears to be fine
- Unacknowledged tensions exist deep below
- Life is chaotic, confusing & unpredictable particularly in the face of unexpected challenges

IN YOUR LIFE:
- There is clear alignment between your inner & outer world
- Nothing is hidden
- You go with ease even in the face of unexpected challenges

As indicated by using a continuum, I realized that self-connection was not an either/or state for me. Instead, depending on my circumstances, I could experience different levels of connection and disconnection. However, I could identify qualities that clearly marked the extreme ends of the continuum. For example, being overly driven by the need for external rewards and recognition meant I had disconnected from my internal needs and desires. Lacking a strong connection to my Internal Wisdom left me open to the whims of others, thereby introducing a certain level of unpredictability and chaos into my life.

With the benefit of hindsight, I can now look at this continuum and place myself firmly on the left-hand side of the continuum at the time of my story.

No wonder I felt so lost!

Now it's Your Turn

The purpose of this exercise is to introduce you to *The Continuum of Self-Connection* and get a general idea of where you might place yourself. Don't over think it. In the rest of this chapter, you will learn much more about the continuum and its important role in helping you to make a YOU Turn. With this understanding in hand, you will revisit this exercise at the end of the chapter.

Exploring Your Level of Self-Connection

Take a look at the qualities describing either end of the continuum.
Place an 'X' on the line which best represents your current situation.

The Continuum of Self-Connection

YOU ARE:
- Driven by external rewards & recognition
- Focused on thinking & reasoning
- Not able to recognize or express feelings
- Not aware of internal sensations or cues
- Not able to describe personal needs

YOU ARE:
- Readily able to access & act from Inner Wisdom
- Able to fully integrate mind & body
- Comfortable expressing a full range of feelings
- Highly aware of personal needs
- Have the capacity to balance your needs with the needs of others

DISCONNECTED   **CONNECTED**

IN YOUR LIFE:
- On the surface all appears to be fine
- Unacknowledged tensions exist deep below
- Life is chaotic, confusing & unpredictable particularly in the face of unexpected challenges

IN YOUR LIFE:
- There is clear alignment between your inner & outer world
- Nothing is hidden
- You go with ease even in the face of unexpected challenges

- Reflect on your reasons for where you placed your 'X'

Guidepost 2: Identifying Your Driving Forces

The question plaguing me was, *How did a smart girl like me get so lost?* I always prided myself on being so aware and having a strong voice of reason. It didn't help when I read that this type of disconnection is referred to as *self-estrangement, and prominent in the life of traumatized people* (Maté, 2022, p.32).

Who me, traumatized? I do not think so. I had what I thought was a pretty normal, uneventful upbringing. I equated trauma with experiencing major significant, negative events or stress such as war, natural disasters, a serious accident, or domestic violence—experiences that can cause *intense physical and psychological stress reactions* (SAMHSA, 2014, p.xix). This perception was reinforced when I read through the ten items listed on the Adverse Childhood Experience questionnaire, a tool widely used to screen for exposure to childhood trauma (ACEsAware, 2022):

- Events of overt humiliation or fear of physical harm;
- Physical abuse;
- Unwanted sexual contact;
- Feelings of not being loved;
- Physical neglect;
- Separation or divorce;
- Exposure to intimate partner violence;
- Alcoholism or drug abuse;
- Mental illness or suicide attempt;
- A family member going to prison.

I did not identify with any of these items and struggled to understand how I could be perceived as a traumatized person. Then I learned that this list was classified as *Big T* trauma. However, there was also something called *little t* trauma. This list included:

- Being bullied by peers;
- Casual but repeated harsh comments of a well-meaning parent;
- Lack of sufficient emotional connection with nurturing adults.

I became slightly uncomfortable as I reviewed this list against my childhood experiences.

My parents had immigrated from Holland to Canada in 1955. My father was primarily focused on his business and providing for his family. He lived by the motto: *I work hard so others don't have to.* Indeed, I couldn't remember a time when we connected on an emotional level. My mother was much more involved in parenting us. However, her main style was to parent us through criticism, always commenting on something we could improve. Her guiding mantra seemed to be: *If I don't criticize you, who will?*

My reflections elevated my discomfort because I reasoned that my parents had lived through World War II and had experienced great hardship; they were doing the best they knew how. I felt like a bad daughter, assigning blame for my struggles to them. But then I read that *Blame is a meaningless concept the moment one understands how suffering in a family system, or even in a community, extends back through generations* (Maté, 2022, p. 35).

As a child of immigrants, I did not know my extended family or their history well, but I did know:

- My mother's parents had divorced when she was 16;
- Her father left her family and was verbally quite cruel to my mom;
- As the middle child of five boys, my father had faced challenges growing up.

This all played out in the dynamic of their relationship. My father was so caught up in his work that he had little time for my mother, and my mother was no doubt overwhelmed by raising four daughters with little support in a new country. I'm sure she was somewhat lost herself.

Seeing their relationship as a product of a greater family system allowed me to set aside any notion of blame. I became much more open to exploring the impact of their dynamic on my upbringing.

As a sensitive child, I sensed my mother's need for support and always tried to be there for her. But being so sensitive, I also became easily overwhelmed by my feelings and could be quite reactive. When I acted out, I was often told to go to my room and not come downstairs until I had a smile on my face. The phrase, *Stop being so sensitive*, became familiar to me. As a result of these *little t* traumas, I learned it was not safe to feel, and, in an effort to be a good daughter, I became very capable of repressing and disconnecting from my own needs. As a result, I ultimately performed in a way that kept my parents happy and met their expectations. With the benefit of hindsight, it is now not difficult to see that I was well on the way to losing myself at a young age.

Even as I write this, I am aware that part of me wants to focus on the fact that my parents provided their four daughters with a very comfortable life. In many ways, I truly wanted for nothing. Nonetheless, I could not deny that my past experiences taught me it was not okay to be who I was or experience what I felt. I believed I was only valuable to the extent of being able to meet the expectations and needs of others. This belief clearly left me vulnerable to becoming codependent, loosing connection with my own needs and priorities along the way.

Now it's Your Turn

Examining your past influences is a necessary step in making a YOU Turn. It helps to unearth experiences that may not be readily obvious to you but are vital in shaping your capacity for self-connection. Depending on your past experiences, you may find his exercise somewhat uncomfortable—as stated in the introduction, please take good care of yourself. If you react strongly, please do not hesitate to seek additional advice and support.

Identifying Your Driving Forces

Trauma is defined as *an inner injury resulting in a lasting rupture or split within the self due to difficult or hurtful events* (Maté, 2022, p. 20).

- Describe your initial reaction to considering the role of trauma in your past. For example, is the idea of trauma new to you, or is it something you have previously been aware of and thought about?

- Consider the lists of experiences included as Big T and little t traumas above and indicate *which resonate with you and why.*

Guidepost 3: Considering Your Outer Influences

In the previous section, you considered how your past experiences can serve as forces driving your level of self-connection. However, you are surrounded by many messages that also strongly influence how you travel through life. Referred to as *Cultural and Societal Context*, these values and beliefs factors make up our outer landscape and influence our capacity for self-connection.

For example, as a young woman growing up in the 60s and 70s, I was surrounded by the message that women could have it all, and yet, I lived in a highly patriarchal society where men held the power and created the rules. In response to this double standard, I internalized the notion that success for a woman was living in a two-career household, owning a house, and accumulating material goods, all while raising a family. There was no question that I could be this *superwoman*, so I merrily completed two master's degrees and a PhD and held down jobs with a high degree of increasing responsibility, all while raising two children.

Maintaining this lifestyle was well supported by my capacity to suppress and ignore my own needs. This was less of a conscious decision on my part, but instead, something that seemed like the right thing to do. Ironically, my well-honed capacity to disconnect from my inner world and to live in my big brain served me very well during this time. It was easy and safe to be driven by logic rather than my feelings. I fit well into academia and could readily navigate driving in a man's world. The trauma or disconnection I experienced growing up was continuously reinforced through my outer landscape.

Now it's Your Turn

Depending on your age and circumstances, you will have encountered any number of different cultural and societal influences throughout your lifetime. For example, the current landscape is marked by the negative impact of colonialism and the experience of climate change. These are just a few conditions contributing to an increasingly distressing and divisive environment. Given these turbulent times, some form of distraction is often employed as a coping strategy. One such distraction is readily reinforced through easy access to social media. Ongoing distraction contributes to a state of disconnection. The following exercise is designed for you to consider how social and cultural conditions influence your level of self-connection.

Considering Your Outer Influences: Cultural & Societal Context

- Describe any current cultural expectations and societal developments you encounter on a regular basis.

- Reflect on how this context influences your capacity for self-connection.

Guidepost 4: Revisiting Your Level of Self-Connection

Working through the guideposts, I realized that my past experiences and outer influences served as significant forces contributing to my capacity for self-connection. As illustrated in the diagram below, I saw these occurrences as part of a wheel that could move me from a state of disconnection or connection, depending on circumstances.

The Continuum of Self-Connection

YOU ARE:
- Driven by external rewards & recognition
- Focused on thinking & reasoning
- Not able to recognize or express feelings
- Not aware of internal sensations or cues
- Not able to describe personal needs

YOU ARE:
- Readily able to access & act from Inner Wisdom
- Able to fully integrate mind & body
- Comfortable expressing a full range of feelings
- Highly aware of personal needs
- Have the capacity to balance your needs with the needs of others

DISCONNECTED ←———————————————————→ **CONNECTED**

IN YOUR LIFE:
- On the surface all appears to be fine
- Unacknowledged tensions exist deep below
- Life is chaotic, confusing & unpredictable particularly in the face of unexpected challenges

IN YOUR LIFE:
- There is clear alignment between your inner & outer world
- Nothing is hidden
- You go with ease even in the face of unexpected challenges

For example, as I reviewed my past, it became clear I had internalized the following messages:

- It is not safe to feel;
- I am only loveable to the extent that I can meet the needs and expectations of others.

To live this way, I had become very capable of suppressing my feelings and Inner Wisdom while constantly scanning the landscape to see how I could serve the needs of others. To make matters worse, this level of disconnection was positively reinforced by living in a patriarchal, accomplishment-driven society.

These messages served as the invisible force that had kept me stuck in my unhealthy situation for so long. On a very deep level, I honestly thought that the way forward was to meet everyone else's needs and expectations, particularly those of my partner. In doing so, I did not realize I had completely lost touch with myself and my Inner Wisdom.

As I looked in my rear-view mirror, it was no wonder that, on the surface, everything appeared to be fine, yet my life was incredibly chaotic. It was like living in a whirlwind without having control over where and when the next gust would hit.

Now it's Your Turn

At the beginning of this chapter, you placed yourself on the continuum based on a general sense of your level of self-connection. This exercise gives you the opportunity to reconsider your initial placement in light of having examined your history and context.

Revisiting Your Level of Self-Connection

As you consider what you learned about yourself in this chapter,
place an X on the Continuum of Self-Connection chart below
that best represents how your Driving Forces have
shaped your level of connection.

The Continuum of Self-Connection

YOU ARE:
- Driven by external rewards & recognition
- Focused on thinking & reasoning
- Not able to recognize or express feelings
- Not aware of internal sensations or cues
- Not able to describe personal needs

DRIVING FORCES:
Past Experiences
- Exposure to Big T and/or little t trauma(s)
- Family history

Cultural & Social Context

YOU ARE:
- Readily able to access & act from Inner Wisdom
- Able to fully integrate mind & body
- Comfortable expressing a full range of feelings
- Highly aware of personal needs
- Have the capacity to balance your needs with the needs of others

DISCONNECTED

CONNECTED

IN YOUR LIFE:
- On the surface all appears to be fine
- Unacknowledged tensions exist deep below
- Life is chaotic, confusing & unpredictable particularly in the face of unexpected challenges

IN YOUR LIFE:
- There is clear alignment between your inner & outer world
- Nothing is hidden
- You go with ease even in the face of unexpected challenges

- Reflect on how this placement compares to your assessment in Exercise #1

In Summary

In Chapter 2, you explored how your life experiences contribute to your level of self-connection.

As you continue your journey, you will learn how to strengthen your capacity for self-connection. At this point, you probably see your dilemma from a different perspective. And the way forward will become much easier to navigate. However, before that happens, ensuring your road ahead is completely open is important. Clearing your path of any existing roadblocks is the focus of Chapter 3.

Insights and Questions

Use this space to capture anything that may have surprised you
while completing Chapter 2 or
something that you may be wondering about as you move into Chapter 3.

Key Concepts

Codependence
Codependence is a complex concept. There is not one universally accepted definition. The following description has been pieced together from a variety of resources listed below.

Codependence is a relationship in which individuals with an undefined sense of self, rely on meeting the needs of another person as a way of fulfilling their own emotional and self-esteem needs. Although originally applied to the partners of alcoholics, research has shown that the characteristics of codependence are also prevalent in the general population, particularly when one is raised in a society that values external validation over internal integrity.

Trauma
An inner injury resulting in a lasting rupture or split within the self, due to difficult or hurtful events (Maté, 2022, p. 20).

- **Big T Trauma**
  Major significant negative events or stress such as war, natural disasters, a serious accident, or domestic violence—experiences that can cause intense physical and psychological stress reactions.

- **little t Trauma**
  Seemingly ordinary events that often do not involve overt distress but reinforce the experience of not being seen or accepted, thereby causing a lasting rejection of and rupture within the self.

The Continuum of Self-Connection
A model representing the notion that the states of disconnection from, and connection to, one's self exist on a continuum and can be present or absent in different degrees, over time, depending on a variety of factors.

References

ACESs Aware. Adverse-Childhood Experience Questionnaire for Adults https://www.acesaware.org/wp-content/uploads/2022/07/ACE-Questionnaire-for-Adults-Identified-English-rev.7.26.22.pdf

Bacon, I.G.F.I. (2015). An exploration of the experience of codependency through interpretive phenomenological analysis. PhD Thesis. Brunel University.

Bacon, I.G.F.I. McKay, E, Reynolds, F and McIntyre, A. (2020). The Lived Experience of codependency: an interpretive phenomenological analysis. International Journal of Mental Health and Addiction. 18(3), pp754-771.

Beattie M. (1992). Codependent No More: How to Stop Controlling Others and Start Caring for Yourself. Second Edition. Centre City: MN, Hazeldon Publishers.

Maté, G. (2022). The Myth of Normal: Trauma & Healing in a Toxic Culture. London, UK: Penguin Random House.

Mellody P. (2003). Facing Codependence: What It Is, Where It Comes From, How It Sabotages Our Lives. New York, NY: HarperCollins Publishers.

Miller, J.K. (1997). Compelled to Control. Recovering Intimacy in Broken Relationships. Deerfield Beach, FL: Health Communications Inc.

Real, T. (2017). The Long Shadow of Trump. Couples Therapy in the Age of Trump. Psychotherapy Networker. September/October, pp34-58.

Real T. (1998). I Don't Want to Talk About It: Overcoming the Secret Legacy of Male Depression. New York, Fireside. 1st Fireside ed.

SAMHSA. Substance Abuse and Mental Health Services Administration. (2014). Trauma Informed Care in Behavioral Health Services. Treatment Improvement protocol (TIP) Series 57. HHS Publication No. (SMA) 14-4816. Rockville, MD: Substance Abuse and Mental Health Administration.

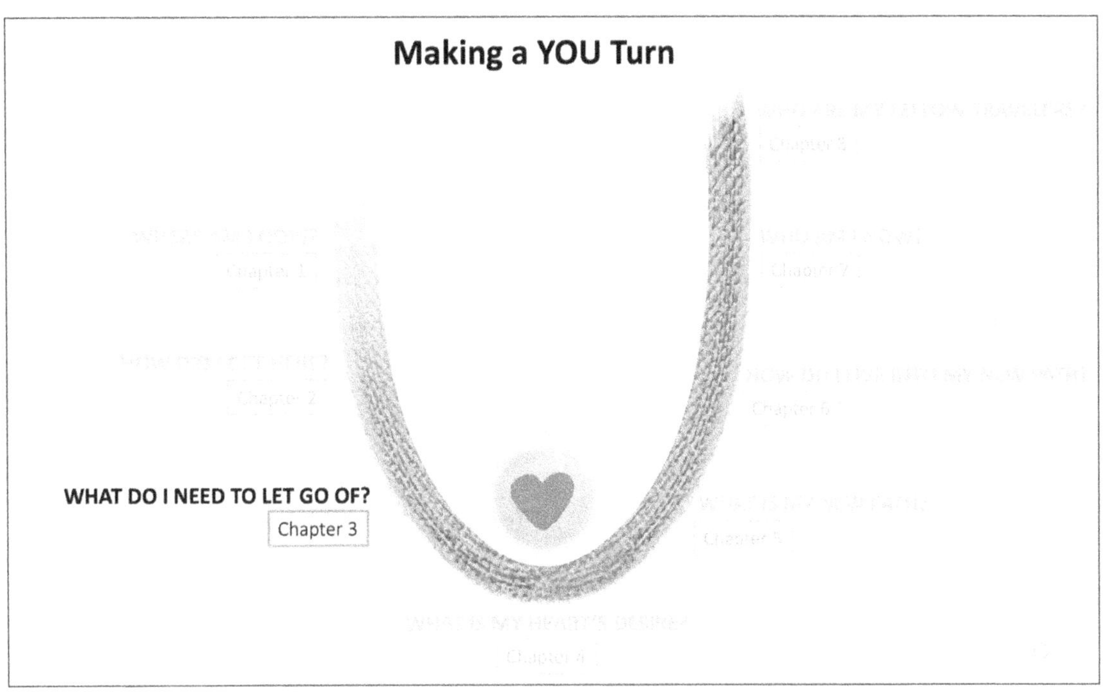

Chapter 3

What Do I Need to Let Go Of

Identifying and Clearing Your Path of Roadblocks

In chapter 2, I introduced The Continuum of Self-Connection. The key to making a YOU Turn is getting the wheel to move towards the right on the continuum—towards living a life where your Inner Wisdom is readily available to guide you smoothly through any crossroad.

It sounds so easy!

However, as you discovered in Chapter 2, life can surround you with messages, allowing external forces to determine your path. Over time, these messages become so entrenched that they can block you from fully accessing your Inner Wisdom. This chapter focuses on identifying and letting go of your roadblock so you can travel your new path unencumbered by any barriers from your past.

My Invitation to You

Developing the capacity to *just let go* is a critical step in eliminating your roadblock. The following story describes my experience of learning to let go—where I stilled my thoughts and allowed my feelings to run quietly in the background.
I felt completely at home in my body and became aware of every sensation without feeling compelled to respond.

As you read my story, please consider the following:

- If you have ever experienced a time when you could completely let go, describe it below. If not, describe what you feel as you consider the possibility.

You will discover in my story that I initially had a strong reaction to the question; *What is here now if there is no problem to solve?*

- Share your reaction as you consider *What is here now if there is no problem to solve?*

Letting Go of Old Baggage:
Preparing for My You Turn

It is the fall of 2018. Driving on a highway in Italy, travelling from Milan to Quarna Sopra, a little town high up in the Italian Alps, I'm on my way to a week-long retreat called Accessing and Living from Self. The brochure promises the experience will help me connect to my core essence. After realizing how disconnected I had become, I know this is just what I need! I am excited to be going.

On the first day, one by one, 40 of us enter the retreat room, a beautiful large open space. We each pull up a chair and form a circle. As the time to start draws near, the friendly chatter gradually dies down, and the room becomes quiet. We begin with a round of introductions. I am torn not knowing how to introduce myself and explain what brought me here. Do I tell the truth and share what has happened over the last two years: how both my parents died, my marriage finally imploded, a very close friend died of pancreatic cancer far too early, and I am estranged from my son and worried about my daughter? Do I include how my usual strategies are not working and I can't seem to fix anything anymore?

Do I add that I came here desperate to find a new way through?

Sharing all this seems far too risky in a room full of strangers. So instead, I tap into my well-developed professional demeanour and describe myself as an Education Scientist, here to learn some new strategies. At least, I hope that's what I said. It all went by in a bit of a blur.

Much to my surprise, the opening session had an immediate impact. Having a double master's in divinity and social work, Loch Kelly is a leader in developing and practicing open-hearted awareness. With sparkling eyes and an impish grin, he stands up and stretches his arms out wide, drawing us all in as if preparing to address his congregation. As he stands, the air in the room becomes immediately energized; I feel pulled into his personal circle. He leans forward, standing on the balls of his feet, and almost but not quite takes a step into the centre of the circle. He invites us to consider the question,

What is here now if there is no problem to solve?

The question hangs in the air. He scans the room with his eyes locking on each of us in turn and repeats the phrase. "What is here now if there is no problem to solve?" The room is so quiet that I could hear a pin drop. I tighten up. I find the question very irritating.

How can there not be a problem to solve?
Does he not live in this world?
Clearly, he does not know my reality.
Things need to be fixed, and problems need to be solved!
That's why I am here!!

Loch repeats the question again and slowly begins engaging in a strange type of dance. Bending his elbows, he brings his fingertips to his temples, which gently rest just above his eyebrows. Then, in a single gesture, he opens his arms. As his fingertips move away from his temples, he utters a single word: "Unhook." Then, he pauses and repeats the gesture and the word: "Unhook." His complete dance is made up of a series of sequential arm gestures accompanied by more single words:

"Drop"
"Open"
"See"
"Include"
"Know"
And finally, the phrase: "Let be."

The entire dance is intended to evoke a shift out of ego, out of the chattering everyday mind, or what he laughingly refers to as "mini-me" into a state of "awake awareness." This state where we can glimpse who we really are— where we experience our Self essence.

He repeats this dance many times over the course of the week, but he has me at "unhook." He repeats the word a second time as he moves his arms away from his head. My head lifts as if powered by some unseen force. I spontaneously take a deep breath, and my whole body relaxes and opens. My eyes soften, my vision expands. I can see my thoughts "unhook" and float away.

This is how I feel when I let go.

Lessons Learned

A roadblock is a barrier set up by authorities, stopping traffic from moving forward. However, unlike a concrete roadblock, a YOU Turn roadblock is much less obvious. It is a belief, carefully curated over time, that operates well below your level of awareness. Once you find it, it becomes crystal clear how this belief contributed to a pattern of behaviour, keeping you in a state of disconnection.

As I continued my journey, I uncovered one particularly significant roadblock which made it difficult to fully access my Inner Wisdom and start my YOU Turn. It was critical for me to remove this roadblock before taking another step. The following four guideposts helped to clear my path:

1. Identifying your roadblock;
2. Letting go of your roadblock;
3. Allowing yourself to grieve;
4. Revisiting your crossroad.

Refresher:
Remembering Your Driving Forces

In Chapter 2, guidepost 2 & 3 required you to consider your Driving Forces:
the influential experiences from your past that have shaped you.
These include:

Past Experiences
• Exposure to trauma
• Family history
Cultural & Social Context

Take a minute to recall and write down any key influences or experiences below.
This information will be helpful as you work through Chapter 3

Guidepost 1: Identifying Your Roadblock

As I reflected on my Driving Forces, it became clear that a significant roadblock was my deeply-entrenched belief that my intellectual skill and well-developed capacity for objective reasoning were the keys to my success—finding just the right reasoning was the key to solving any problem. Given this belief, it is not hard to see why I developed the assumption that if I thought long and hard enough, I could fix my husband, love would prevail, and we would all live happily ever after. THE END.

My belief in this Hollywood ending turned out to be my biggest roadblock.

Martha Stark (2017) so brilliantly refers to this pattern of behaviour as *Relentless Hope*. It is the belief that all will be well by forcing someone else to change rather than directly dealing with the pain of a difficult situation. Finding ways to make someone or something else change becomes the focus, even though, despite using different strategies, the desired result does not materialize.

Over time, I characterized my behaviour as engaging in a cycle of relentless hope. I continuously thought of different strategies to try to fix my husband and the situation. That's how strongly I believed in the power of my reasoning and in the possibility of a perfect Hollywood ending. Not surprisingly, this cycle reminds me of one definition of insanity: doing the same thing repeatedly and expecting different results. It was definitely time to move on.

Now it's Your Turn

This exercise provides you with the opportunity to explore any roadblocks or beliefs that might be keeping you stuck. Depending on where you are in your journey, your roadblocks might be readily apparent, or they might take some time to uncover. Start with what is most obvious to you at this moment in time. As with all these exercises, you can revisit and refine your responses whenever a new insight emerges.

Identifying Your Roadblock

- As you consider your situation, describe any roadblocks or beliefs that might be keeping you from moving on.

- Identify a roadblock that stands out as being particularly significant.

Guidepost 2: Letting Go of Your Roadblock

Naming your roadblock is one thing but being able to let go is another. Even when I wrote the notion above that *love would prevail*, I could feel a part of me wanting to believe in the magic of my *Hollywood ending*. Thankfully, during my experience at the retreat, I learned what it felt like to *unhook and let go*. So, over time, whenever I became aware of my roadblock appearing, I took a moment to lift my head, pause, and watch my belief float away.

However, like a physical barrier, some YOU Turn roadblocks can be as solid as concrete. It takes great strength to name this kind of belief, let alone start the process of letting go. My real motivation arrived when I finally came face-to-face with the consequence of my behaviour.

My Story Continues

Halfway through my retreat week, I receive a text from my daughter, "Mom, I need to talk to you." My stomach tenses, and I sigh heavily. She never texts me, so I automatically anticipate some news about my partner. We had separated a year earlier in the fall of 2017, but he seemed intent on getting help. He appeared to have rallied since our separation, and I continued holding hope for my Hollywood ending. He offered to come over to the house to help care for the dogs during my stay in Italy, and I gladly accepted. I thought this was a good sign.

After dinner, I go to the library to call my daughter, "Dad started drinking again the second you left." I let her words sink in, and moving into action mode, I quickly reply, "I can come home." 'She answers, "No, I know you need this time away, and I can take care of myself, but I need you to talk to Dad and tell him not to come to the house anymore." My heart breaks hearing the distress in her voice. At that moment I clearly recognize that my need to believe in a perfect ending has come at the expense of my children.

I lift my head as if powered by some unseen force. My whole body relaxes and opens as I take a deep breath—my eyes soften, my vision expands.

I see my Hollywood ending unhook and begin to float away.

Now it's Your Turn

As described in my story, the realization that my children were suffering because of my behaviour was instrumental in starting my process of letting go. Recognizing the negative consequences of hanging on to a roadblock is a critical step in letting go and moving on. There can be many different consequences depending on your situation. For example, your consequence may not involve others but may harm your ability to fulfill your needs and desires. Depending on your consequence, you might be tempted to go into a blame mode . Be aware of the would'ves, could'ves should'ves . Be gentle with yourself as you complete this exercise.

Letting Go of Your Roadblock

- List and describe the negative consequences you might be experiencing by hanging on to your roadblock.

- Is there one consequence that stands out as being most important?

Guidepost 3: Allowing Yourself to Grieve

One advantage of believing in my Hollywood ending is that I could continue my finely honed practice of repressing any pain or anger I felt as my marriage fell apart. Not surprisingly, as I began letting go of my Hollywood ending, my feelings simultaneously started to surface. As I realized that I could not save my partner or my marriage, the sadness and grief that had been accumulating over the years began to emerge. This grief was compounded by the loss of my parents, close friend, and connection to my children.

My story continues

Being completely on my own, far away from home, I hear the universe tell me, "It's time to remember, to grieve, and to let go." As I wander through town, I come upon an old church, The Church of Santo Stephano. I enter a graveyard behind the church, and I'm struck by the elaborate headstones holding pictures reminding me of the lives that once were. Mausoleums circle the cemetery where families are laid to rest together. These sacred structures form a wall around the graveyard, protecting the deceased. I find a spot in a corner where I am slightly hidden from sight but can see everything. I observe an elderly woman lovingly tends to one of the gravesites. As I settle in, my head lifts to the sky as if powered by an unseen force. My eyes soften, and tears slowly begin to flow.

The grief I have been holding on to begins to unhook and float away.

Now it's Your Turn

Suppressed grief is energy that allows you to hold on to your old beliefs and ways of doing things. It is common to be afraid of being overwhelmed as you think of releasing the amount of grief that you may be holding on to. Here is an exercise that will help you surrender to
your grief without the fear of being swamped.

Allowing Yourself to Grieve

To do this exercise you will need a quiet spot, paper, pencil, a match,
and a bowl or container you can burn the paper in.

- Write down your roadblock on a piece of paper.

- Find a quiet spot.

- Hold on to the paper, and ask yourself, *Where am I holding on to my grief in my body?*

- As you consider this question, close your eyes and slow your breathing while doing an internal body scan from your feet to the top of your head and back again.

- If an image arises, be a silent observer. For example, when I asked myself this question, my grief showed up as an ice block surrounding my heart. As I breathed into this image, I saw the ice start to melt. Not surprisingly, this was accompanied by a gentle flow of tears. After a period of time, my tears naturally stopped flowing. At that point, I opened my eyes, burned my piece of paper, and invited myself to *Just. Let. Go.*

Please remember that letting go of grief is a process.
This exercise is designed to help you let go gradually over time.
You can do this exercise as often as you need.

Guidepost 4: Revisiting Your Crossroad

Should I stay or should I go? This question defined the crossroad that started my journey. Identifying my roadblock, finally understanding the consequence of my behaviour, discovering how much I had disconnected from myself and my Inner Wisdom to stay in my marriage, and ultimately realizing the impact on my children made the answer to my question very clear—it was time to move on.

Although I was very aware that this was not a decision to be taken lightly, I nonetheless felt lighter. I was aware of holding myself differently. As the tension in my shoulders eased, I started sitting up straighter and moving with more ease. A spaciousness emerged as I considered my next steps.

Yes, I knew that moving on from my marriage would continue to be overwhelming at times. However, I realized that I was increasingly experiencing moments of connection to my Inner Wisdom throughout my journey. Moments that Loch so beautifully described as *little glimpses of self-essence*. Within these moments, I was calm and simply curious about what would happen next. But these times still seemed few and far between. It seemed that my journey was far from over as I considered:

How can I continue my journey toward self-connection?

I found myself standing at a new crossroad.

Now it's Your Turn

Letting go of beliefs that no longer serve you paves the way for new insights to emerge. These insights may cause you to see your dilemma and crossroad in a different light. Accordingly, this exercise invites you to revisit, and if appropriate, rewrite or refine the crossroad articulated at the beginning of your journey.

Revisiting Your Crossroad

- Write down the crossroad you identified in Chapter 1, Guidepost 2.

- Considering the insights gained in your journey so far, reflect on whether or not your crossroad is still accurate or if it has evolved. Rewrite or refine your crossroad as appropriate.

In Summary

In Chapter 3, you identified and let go of a significant roadblock. A roadblock keeps you from making a YOU Turn by creating a barrier to tuning into your priorities and desires. By letting go, you create space for your Inner Wisdom to emerge. Fully connecting to your Inner Wisdom is the focus of Chapter 4.

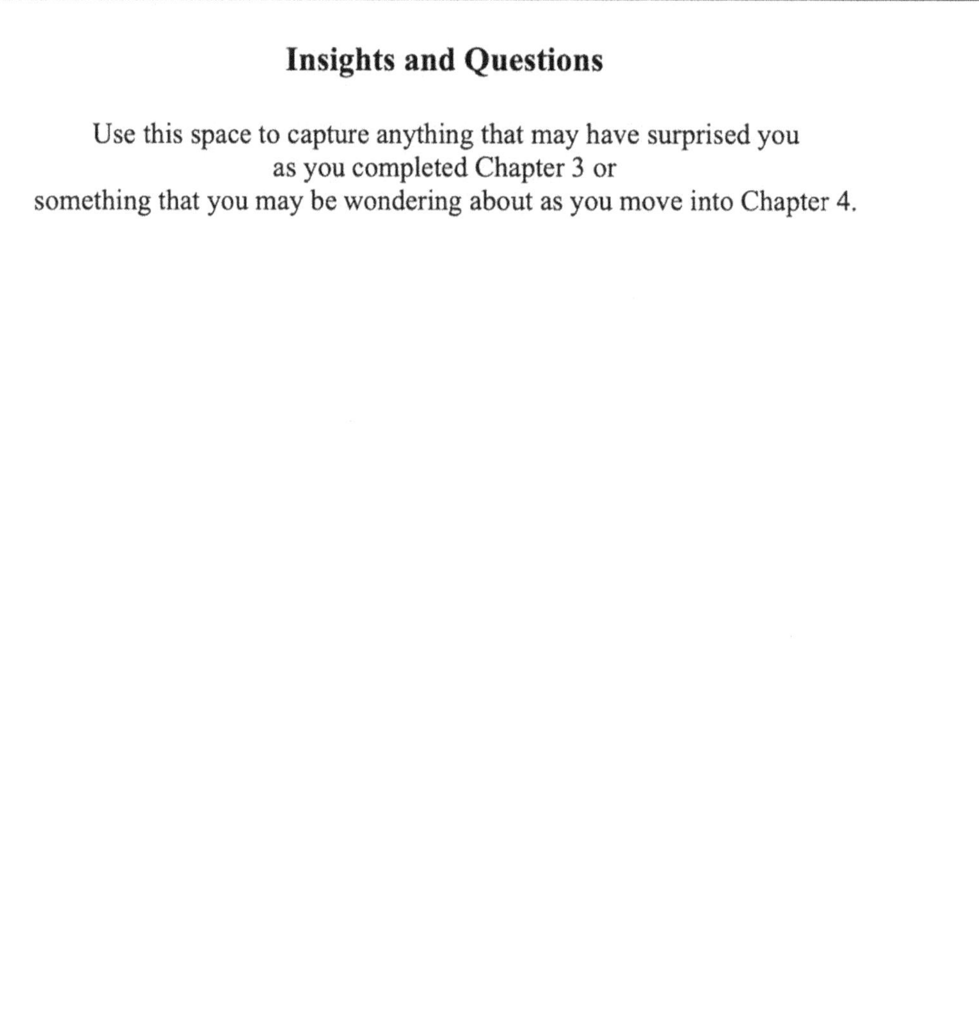

Key Concepts

Hollywood Ending
An ending in a movie or a novel for example, that is full of unrealistic, exaggerated happiness or love.

Relentless Hope
The mistaken belief that all will be well once you can get someone else to change. It stems from an inability to directly examine and deal with the pain of a difficult situation. The experience is labelled relentless because the individual insists on persisting with attempting to make the other person change, even though the desired result never materializes.

Roadblock
A belief, carefully curated over time, that operates well below your level of awareness and contributes to a pattern of behaviour that keeps you in an ongoing state of disconnection.

References

Kelly L. (2015) Shift into Freedom: The science and practice of open-hearted awareness. Boulder CO: Sounds True Publishers.

Stark M. (2017). Relentless Hope: The refusal to grieve. E-Book International Psychotherapy Institute. Available at: https://www.freepsychotherapybooks.org/ebook/relentless-hope-2/

Chapter 4

What is My Heart's Desire?

Taking a Deep Dive into Your Inner Wisdom

In Chapter 3, you focused on letting go of messages, beliefs, and patterns of behaviour that no longer serve you. Letting go creates the space for you to allow new beliefs and behaviours in—actions that align more with your heart's desire.

Your heart's desire speaks to your intention for your life. It fuels your purpose and ultimately sustains you. It has always been with you but is often overshadowed by external events and expectations. Strengthening your connection to your Inner Wisdom allows you to listen to your heart's desire. Chapter 4 focuses on how to make this happen.

As you can see from the diagram above, finding your Heart's Desire is exactly what you need to make a YOU Turn. Congratulations on making it this far.

You are now entering the best part of your journey.

52

My Invitation to You

Accessing and acting from your Inner Wisdom is a key step in making a You Turn.
The following story describes how listening to this inner voice
provided significant insight into my heart's desire.

As you read my story, see if you can put yourself in my shoes. Imagine what it would be like
to be in a safe and welcoming space where you are free to find your spark and connect to
your heart's desires. Describe what that space looks like for you.

Finding My Spark:
Moving from Fear into Love

It is the spring of 2019. I am one of ten women scattered around a large room in a beautiful Lake Tahoe waterfront home. The view is nothing short of spectacular. The sun is shining, the sky is clear, the water is a deep blue, and the mountains rise majestically on the other side of the lake. However, no one is taking in the view at this particular moment. The room is completely silent, and all eyes look down as we focus on the task at hand.

We just started a three-day retreat entitled 'The Remarkable Women's Journey', a six-month program that promises to 'empower you to take the next evolutionary leap and design the best decade of your life'. We range in age from 45 to 67, and at 62, I am one of the older participants. But age doesn't seem to matter because we are all here for the same reason; we all have a fierce desire to affirm our unique stand so we can be of service to the world—whatever form that might take. After my experience in Italy, I am ready to find my stand.

We are halfway through this retreat, and everyone has told their personal story. The ice is broken, a level of comfort is established, and we are ready to get to work. Based on the adage 'Who you are is where you stand', our lead facilitator, Lynne Twist, invites us to write a statement that captures our inner desire: a statement that guides us without creating sides or judgment. My pen flies over the page as I write effortlessly and with great enthusiasm:

**I stand for the possibilities that emerge when
we consciously choose to live through the energy of love and not fear.**

The words don't surprise me. I recently allowed myself to take a deep dive into my heart's desire. During this time, I became acutely aware of the danger of letting my anger and fear of being alone turn into chronic bitterness. I realized that this state would serve no one, and so living through love became the only choice for me. Although part of me worried I was simply replacing one unattainable 'Hollywood Ending' with another, and I didn't have a clue as to how to live through love and not fear, somehow, the words resonated through every cell in my body.

It was time to follow my Inner Wisdom.

Lessons Learned

Finding your heart's desire is a critical step in making a YOU Turn. Your heart's desire speaks to who you are. This step is where you begin to clarify your new direction. It is literally where the rubber hits the road as you turn your steering wheel towards living a full and connected life.

The following four guideposts proved to be essential as I navigated my own YOU Turn.

1. Creating safety;
2. Articulating your heart's desire;
3. Connecting to your Inner Wisdom;
4. Celebrating your progress.

Refresher:
Letting Go of What No Longer Serves You

In Chapter 3, you let go of a roadblock or belief
that was getting in the way of you making your YOU Turn.

Take a minute to remember and write down your roadblock.

Be aware of any time this roadblock comes up as you work through Chapter 4.
Anytime this happens, take a minute to *just let go*.

Use this strategy whenever any thoughts arise that cause you to question the possibility
and/or the importance of finding your heart's desire.

Guidepost 1: Creating Safety

I felt anxious as I let go of old beliefs and created room for something new to emerge. I had lived for such a long time guided by external expectations, driven by the need to take action, and feeling like I always had to be doing something that I didn't know how to sit with the spaciousness of letting go. My tension was palpable; I experienced a hollow pit in my stomach as I struggled not to return to my old ways.

I recognized that being somewhat off balance as I struggled to find a new way through was necessary at this stage in my journey. Creating a sense of safety so I could allow for these uncomfortable sensations to arise without immediately responding became an important strategy. The Remarkable Women's Journey provided that space for me.

From the moment I entered the retreat, I experienced:

- A physically comfortable and welcoming environment;
- Connection to nature;
- Nourishing food;
- Supportive, non-judgmental facilitators;
- Unconditional acceptance from fellow participants;
- Opportunities for joyful play;
- Time for stillness and reflection.

It was no wonder that during the retreat, I could so clearly hear and connect to my Inner Wisdom.

Later, I learned that maximizing cues of safety keeps our nervous system from entering a state of defence (Porges, 2017). Otherwise referred to as *fight, flight, or freeze*, taking a defensive stance bars the way to making a solid connection to your inner world. Therefore, creating safety is a necessary condition for entering into a supportive state so you can find and listen to your heart's desire. Clearly the retreat conditions had created this safe environment for me.

Now it's Your Turn

There is no question that meditating is one practice that helps to facilitate inner connection. However, there are many ways to create safety as you go about your day (Dana, 2020). The following exercise is designed to help you discover the breadth of conditions that enable you to access your Inner Wisdom as you turn your attention fully inward.

Creating Safety

You can experience cues of safety under different circumstances.
Below are questions to help create a list of conditions
that will foster safety specifically for you.

- What physical spaces invite stillness and connection to me?
- Who makes me feel safe and welcome?
- What sounds, smells, and sights bring me comfort? For example, music or nature.
- When have I felt completely at ease? Describe this moment.

Use the following space to create your list of conditions as you reflect on your answers.

Your imagination is a powerful tool. The beauty of creating this list will support you to
recognize that you don't need to be in a particular situation to experience safety. Sometimes,
it's enough to draw one specific time or experience into your memory. For example, when I
close my eyes and reimagine my time at the retreat, my body becomes still,
my breathing slows, and, once again, I connect to my Inner Wisdom.

Take a moment to review your list and experience what happens.

Guidepost 2: Articulating Your Heart's Desire

This is a pivotal step in making a You Turn—finding a new destination, something that inspires you to make a radical shift out of

old ways of doing into new ways of being.

I wish I could provide you with a perfect formula for taking this step, but it is more like deciding that you want to go on a trip but not being sure where you want to go. I knew I needed to leave how I had been living behind, so I began finding resources—travel brochures in a sense—and immersed myself in new experiences to find a new destination. Over time, the shift I desired began to emerge.

Referring back to Chapter 2 and my driving forces, I understood that I had been living in a state of fear. My past experiences taught me to fear my feelings, to fear that I was not loveable for who I am. Also, given the increasing global unrest, fear was an incessant, insidious part of my everyday environment. As I reflected on the Continuum of Self-Connection, it became clear that

living in fear kept me in a state of disconnection.

As I consulted different resources and widened my understanding, I noticed that living through love was consistently offered as the antidote to living in fear. Initially, having been educated in a scientific tradition, living through love seemed far too intangible and *out there* to me. Perhaps it was good in theory, but what did it really mean in practice? Then, I came across the work of Teilhard de Chardin (Savary & Berne, 2017). As a Jesuit scientist, Teilhard was a well-respected paleontologist. During his lifetime, from 1881 to 1955, in addition to many other scientific accomplishments, he explored the philosophy of love. He presented love as a force within us, driving the want to make a positive difference in the world. He proposed that love is the core energy of an evolving life and the divine spark in each of us, waiting to be cultivated and developed until it matures. He advocated that, like other scientifically-studied energy sources, love energy needed to be studied as a power for individual and social transformation. I was mesmerized.

I wanted to understand and, perhaps more importantly, experience how I could shift from living in fear to living through the energy of love. Consequently, my words came quickly when invited to take a stand at the retreat.

I stand for the possibilities that emerge when
we consciously choose to live through the energy of love and not fear.

This was my new destination. To learn to live through the energy of love.

Now it's Your Turn

The following exercise is designed to help you map out where you stand. If you are early on in your journey, you may find this challenging. Please do not aim for perfection or crystal clarity the first time around. Simply use this exercise to begin generating some ideas. You will have many opportunities to return to, revise, refine, and build on your ideas and destination as your YOU Turn continues.

Your destination is a statement that encompasses every aspect of your being. It captures a way of moving forward that aligns completely with your priorities and passions. For example, understanding how I could shift from living in fear to living through the energy of love aligned perfectly with my inner drive and capacity. I had the scientific background and training to embrace the exploration of love as an energy force. Combined with my growing desire to connect to my heart's desire, it is no wonder that pursuing this destination resonated with every cell in my body.

Articulating Your Heart's Desire:
Taking a Stand

A stand is a statement that represents your inner spark—words that affirm what is truly important to you. Your statement is not open to debate. For example, it is not about stating your position in relation to someone else's or creating a statement with which someone can agree or disagree. Instead, it represents what is important to you.

I Stand For ____.

Find the words that work best for you at this moment.

Once you are satisfied,
write your stand on a cue card and keep it close at hand.

Guidepost 3: Tuning Into Your Inner Wisdom

Throughout this journey, you have been invited to tap into your Inner Wisdom. In Chapter 1, Guidepost 3, you identified two strategies that allowed you to connect to your Inner Wisdom. In Chapter 2, you were encouraged to draw from this wisdom as you completed the exercises. The purpose of Chapter 3 was to let go of any roadblocks keeping you from accessing your Inner Wisdom.

Now it's time to really focus on finding your Inner Wisdom and putting this voice firmly in the driver's seat. It might be helpful to think of your Inner Wisdom as your inner compass pointing you in the right direction as you continue on your YOU Turn.

Your Inner Wisdom speaks from a place deep inside of you. It differs from speaking through your head or intellect (Conner, 2008).

- Your head voice tends to be:
- Based on a reasoned argument;
- Interested in attaining a particular outcome;
- Always scanning for reactions.

Whereas your Inner Wisdom:

- Speaks straight from your heart;
- Is interested in telling what is uniquely true for you;
- Acts based on what is in front of you right now.

Your Inner Wisdom will tell you if your stand and destination are true for you.

For example, as I reviewed my stand, my head voice was uncomfortable with the notion of living through the energy of love. After all, I reasoned, *What did it mean to live through the energy of love? Where was the scientific evidence that this would help me to make an authentic connection rather than pay lip service to something new?* Most decidedly, my head voice was also worried that my friends and family would think I had become unmoored, or at the very least, had been engaging in some wishful thinking, relying on something as ethereal as the energy of love.

But when I listened to my Inner Wisdom, I heard nothing but wise advice and affirmation.

For example, driven by my belief that *I can fix anything*, I had done a lot of reading, trying to understand alcoholism. I was motivated by a part of me that thought if I could figure out the cause, I could find a fix. Clearly, that did not happen. However, I did learn that traumatized people often turn to some form of addiction to ease their pain. Seeing my now ex-partner through this light made me realize that turning to him in bitterness and anger would not help us move forward or do justice to our more than 30-year history together. It made sense to me that tapping into the energy of love was a better way through. However, beyond knowing I was not speaking of romantic love, I didn't have a clue as to what living through the energy of love meant for me. Nonetheless, my Inner Wisdom told me I had the skills and motivation to figure it out. Although I knew I still had a long way to go, there was no question I had to try out my new stand.

Now it's Your Turn

Your Inner Wisdom speaks most clearly from a place of safety. Start by consulting the list of conditions you created in Guidepost 1 in this chapter and find your place of safety. This can be a space where you can sit quietly without being disturbed or a sense of internal stillness you can tap into regardless of what is happening around you.

Tuning into Your Inner Wisdom

- In this space of safety, read your stand created in Guidepost 2.

  I stand for ____

- Describe how your Head Voice is responding.

- What advice is your Inner Wisdom telling you?

- If it seems appropriate at this point, refine your stand:

  I stand for ____

Guidepost 4: Celebrating Your Progress

Finding my heart's desire was a significant turning point for me. As I looked in my rear-view mirror, I could appreciate that the following milestones were important accomplishments:

- Embracing that it was I who needed to change;
- Facing my dilemma;
- Clarifying my crossroad;
- Examining my driving forces;
- Accepting the consequences of my actions;
- Learning to let go;
- Creating safety;
- Strengthening my connection to my Inner Wisdom.

As I returned to the Continuum of Self-Connection, it became clear that these milestones had helped me to make significant progress on my journey towards self-connection.

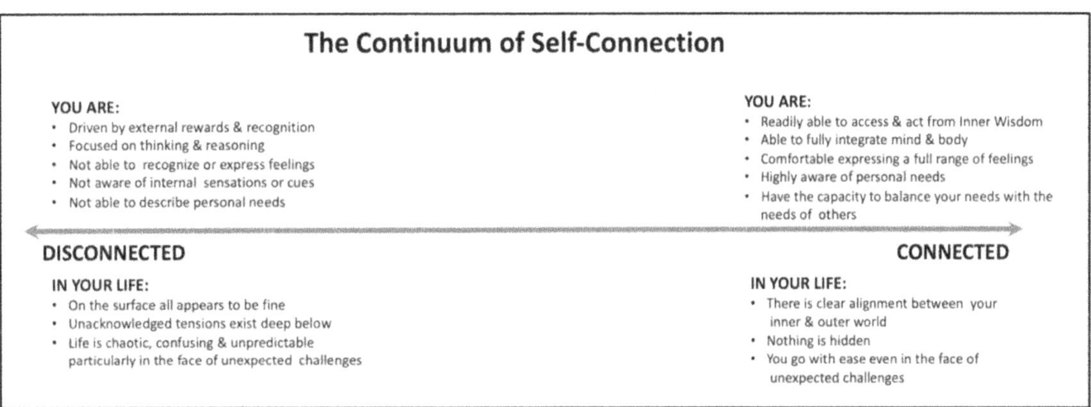

At the beginning of my You Turn, I placed myself firmly on the left-hand side of the continuum. I had become so good at meeting the needs and expectations of others that I lacked an inner compass to help me navigate the difficulties of my marriage. Anyone looking at my life from the outside would probably have assumed that all was fine, yet I was lost and confused about how to move forward. My well-honed strategy of trying to fix everything was no longer working.

Starting with the challenge that I needed to change, helped me let go of the beliefs and actions that no longer served me. As I let go, I was able to let in and strengthen my connection to my Inner Wisdom—the voice that speaks for and from my heart's desire, allowing me to express my unique stand in this world.

It was time to celebrate my progress.

Now it's Your Turn

It is time to pause and celebrate your progress on this journey. Your milestones may be different from mine, but I have no doubt you have experienced several insights along the way. This exercise is designed for you to identify your significant milestones and to appreciate how far you have come.

Celebrating Your Progress

- Take a few minutes to refer back to the work you have accomplished since you started your YOU Turn. Capture your milestones here:

- As you consider the Continuum of Self-Connection, write a few words that capture your starting point and where you are now.

The Continuum of Self-Connection

YOU ARE:
- Driven by external rewards & recognition
- Focused on thinking & reasoning
- Not able to recognize or express feelings
- Not aware of internal sensations or cues
- Not able to describe personal needs

DRIVING FORCES:

Past Experiences
- Exposure to Big T and/or little t trauma(s)
- Family history

Cultural & Social Context

YOU ARE:
- Readily able to access & act from Inner Wisdom
- Able to fully integrate mind & body
- Comfortable expressing a full range of feelings
- Highly aware of personal needs
- Have the capacity to balance your needs with the needs of others

DISCONNECTED

IN YOUR LIFE:
- On the surface all appears to be fine
- Unacknowledged tensions exist deep below
- Life is chaotic, confusing & unpredictable particularly in the face of unexpected challenges

CONNECTED

IN YOUR LIFE:
- There is clear alignment between your inner & outer world
- Nothing is hidden
- You go with ease even in the face of unexpected challenges

- Write a few words of appreciation to yourself for having the courage to go on this journey.

In Chapter 4, you took a deep dive into your heart's desire. Connecting to your Inner Wisdom helped you find and affirm your stand. Continuing to strengthen your capacity for self-connection is the key to living into your heart's desire. This is the focus of Chapter 5.

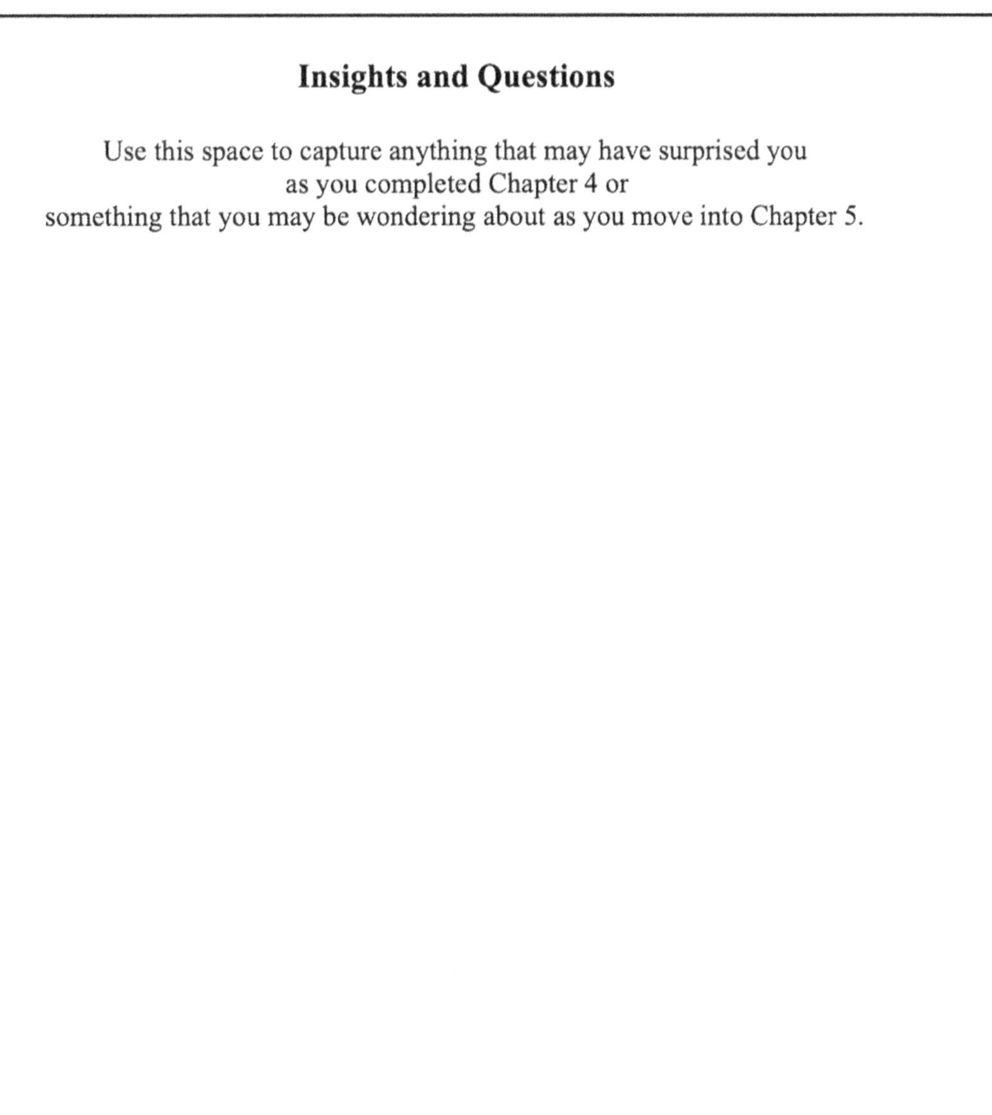

Key Concepts

Cues of Safety
The qualities of an environment that allow one to focus on inner experiences.

Heart's Desire
Something that you long for that when fulfilled creates a deeper and more meaningful connection to self and others.

Inner Wisdom
An inner voice that you can trust to guide you in the right direction.

Stand
A statement that articulates your heart's desire and therefore serves to drive and sustain you by capturing your life's purpose (See Twist, 2017, p. 203-203).

References

Conner, J. (2008). Writing Down Your Soul. How to Activate and Listen to the Extraordinary Voice from Within. San Francisco, CA: Conari Press.

Dana D. (2020). Polyvagal Exercises for Safety and Connection. 50 Client-centered Practices. New York, NY: W.W. Norton & Company, Inc.

Porges S. (2017). The Pocket Guide to Polyvagal Theory. The Transformative Power of Feeling Safe. New York, NY: W.W. Norton & Company, Inc.

Savary L.M. and Berne P.H. (2017). Teilhard de Chardin On Love: Evolving Human Relationships. New York, NY: Paulist Press.

Twist L. (2017). The Soul of Money. Transforming Your Relationship with Money and Life. New York, NY: W.W. Norton & Company Inc.

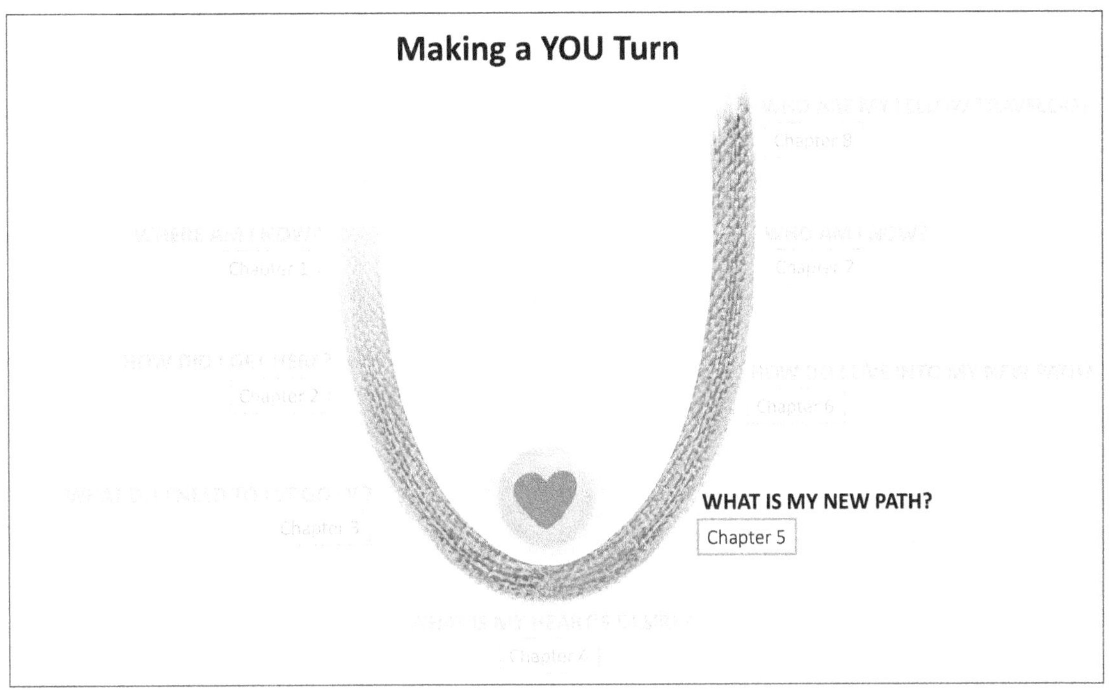

Chapter 5

What is My New Path?

Building Capacity for Self-Awareness Through Sensing, Feeling, and Acting

The first half of this workbook was about examining and shifting your beliefs.
These exercises paved the way for you to find your Inner Wisdom and heart's desire.

Living into your heart's desire relies on experiencing an inner shift. This shift happens when your mind and body work together in complete harmony. At that moment, you are completely present, moving with ease, and fully confident that the steps you are taking are right for you.

The second half of the workbook is about creating the conditions to support this inner transformation as you continue along your new path. In particular, this chapter focuses on building capacity for self-awareness—a critical foundation for your ongoing journey. A word of advice: there is roadwork ahead! Thischapter requires slowing down so you can absorb new ways to travel.
Take your time and enjoy the scenery.

My Invitation to You

The story below describes my experience as I began exploring my heart's desire.
It illustrates the importance of becoming aware of and connecting to
what's happening inside of you, your bodily sensations, thoughts and feelings,
as you find and stay on your new path.

While reading my story, reflect on the following:

- How aware are you of what's happening inside you, your bodily sensations, thoughts and feelings, as you go about your daily activities?

- Describe your reaction to the inner shift I describe in my story. Have you experienced something similar? If so, when and under what circumstances? If not, how do you feel about the possibility of an inner shift?

Finding My Path:
On the Road to Self-Awareness

It is the spring of 2020. I am back at my cottage in Tremblant. It is the perfect place to start bringing my stand to life. Having gathered all my resources, I've allowed myself time to start carving out my new path. I don't have a clue where this road will take me, but I am eager to begin.

After a good night's sleep on this first day, I am walking up the stairs to the main floor. The room comes into view, and my eyes immediately rest on a large table rich in the contours and colours of reclaimed barn board. Originally purchased as a centrepiece to host family and friends, today, it serves as a solid platform for the mountain of books, notes, and papers I've collected over the past year to help me delve into my burning question…

What exactly does it look like and feel like to live through the energy of love and not fear?

My thoughts immediately kick into gear when my feet land on the main floor; I'm as excited as a kid in a candy store. For years, living in my big brain has served me well. This dance of playing with new ideas is very familiar and immediately draws me in. I take a step towards the table, and for some reason, I pause, close my eyes, and consider what is happening at this moment.

I become acutely aware that, as my thoughts engage, all my attention and energy flow upwards, and I lose awareness of any feelings or bodily sensations. It is as if a damper has been drawn.

No wonder the dance feels so familiar. I am repeating a well-worn pattern. My books serve as a cozy blanket, keeping me safely disconnected from any awareness of my inner state. I smile ruefully, realizing this is the typical strategy I developed long ago to protect myself from feeling. Ironically, I become clear that this is what it looks and feels like when I live in fear—being afraid to show up and fully seen for who I am; relying on my books for self-protection.

I give myself some grace.

After all, we are at the beginning of a worldwide pandemic. During my drive to the cottage, a state of lockdown was declared. The world is in turmoil. Although I know how incredibly fortunate I am and that my loved ones are safe, it is impossible not to get caught up in the fear and uncertainty of the times. My cozy blanket of books provides me with much-needed familiarity and a safe space to land.

Nonetheless, I go ahead and clear the table. This is my time to seek guidance from within and not immerse myself in the wisdom of others. As the piles disappear, I become aware of an inner shift, and any tension I hold in my body releases. My feet move with ease as I continue rearranging my space. My eyes soften as my focus turns inward.

I have begun my new path.

Lessons Learned

Travelling a new path depends on your capacity to tap into your bodily sensations, thoughts, and feelings, or what I call your inner landscape. It is not about doing or taking specific steps but rather about being aware of what is happening inside you. This knowledge serves as your personal inner geographic positioning system—iGPS. Your iGPS guides you in knowing when your outer actions are completely in tune with your Inner Landscape. You will know this has happened when you move forward with confidence and ease. Creating this alignment keeps you on your path. In other words, acting from *the inside out* is how your heart's desire becomes a reality.

I learned that this is typically not a well-developed skill. It requires intentionally focusing on building and expanding one's capacity for self-awareness.

Self-awareness is *the ability to monitor your inner world—knowing the relationship between your thoughts, feelings, and reactions* (Goleman,2020, p.269). Self-awareness is critical to ensuring that your actions fully align with what really matters to you (Goleman, 1998). As illustrated in the diagram below, I have come to appreciate that becoming self-aware involves three components whereby:

- *Sensing* refers to the quality of your internal bodily sensations;
- *Feeling* indicates how your mind interprets your bodily sensations;
- *Acting* involves the behaviour that arises when you respond to a particular feeling
- and/or bodily sensation.

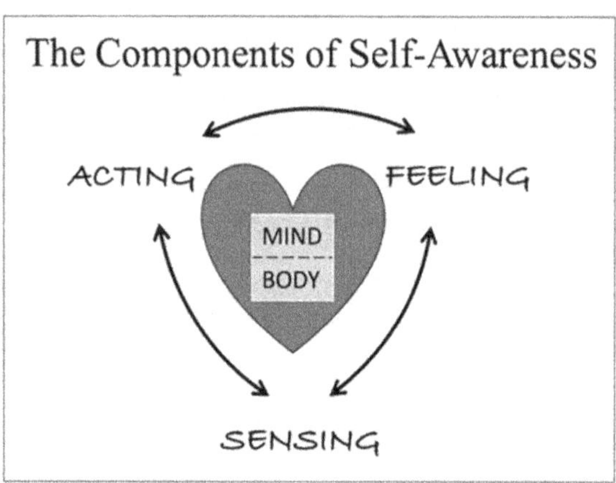

The first three guideposts help you become familiar with each individual component.

However, the diagram is somewhat misleading, since self-awareness doesn't really unfold in a stepwise fashion. Instead, the three components, sensing, feeling, and acting, are intimately intertwined. Consequently, the fourth guidepost describes how self-awareness promotes the experience of alignment between the three components. Alignment happens when your actions fully correspond with your feelings and sensations. It can occur in the blink of an eye and is often experienced as an Inner Shift as your mind and body fully connect.

Accordingly, the guideposts for this chapter are as follows:

1. Tapping into your inner sensations;
2. Describing the role of feelings;
3. Making the connection to actions;
4. Experiencing your inner shift.

As you travel through this chapter, it is important to remember that this is very subtle work. Initially, the process may be quite murky and hard to put into words. You may find yourself going back and forth between guideposts. You may even want to start with the fourth guidepost so you can better understand the Inner Shift and then work backwards through the first three guideposts. No matter how you approach this chapter, you will likely experience increasing moments of insight and clarity; the moments when your iGPS is fully on-line and you have a clear path to your Inner Wisdom. Take your time and be patient as you learn how self-awareness can help you travel your new path.

Refresher:
Articulating Your Heart's Desire

You focused on finding your inner spark in chapter 4—words
that affirm what is truly important to you.
You also created your stand, which represents your inner spark.

As a reminder, take a minute to write your stand below:

As you complete the exercises below, your stand will serve as a touchpoint
as you take the steps to develop and strengthen your capacity for self-awareness.

Guidepost 1: Tapping into Your Inner Sensations

Sensations provide descriptions of what is happening within your physical body. The capacity to tap into these sensations is critical to developing your inner geographic positioning system—iGPS. For example, in my story, I describe how I became skilled at putting a damper on any inner sensations. This allowed me to focus primarily on my thoughts. If you had asked me to describe an inner sensation during certain times in my life, I would have drawn a blank. However, over time, I came to appreciate the importance of becoming attuned to my physical self. I am now aware that my eyes softening is the cue that I am turning inward and connecting to my inner sensations.

As illustrated in the diagram and chart below, once you turn your gaze inward, the physical body provides endless ways to tap into your inner sensations. Your facial expressions, your heart rate, the quality of your breathing, your digestive system, and your muscle condition all provide clues. Most importantly, how your inner landscape unfolds is entirely unique to you. For example, when I experience tension in my jaw, I know I am experiencing some type of difficulty. At times, this difficulty can be accompanied with an uncomfortable twinge just below my breastbone, in my solar plexus. This awareness provides a starting point for me to explore what is happening that is contributing to these inner sensations.

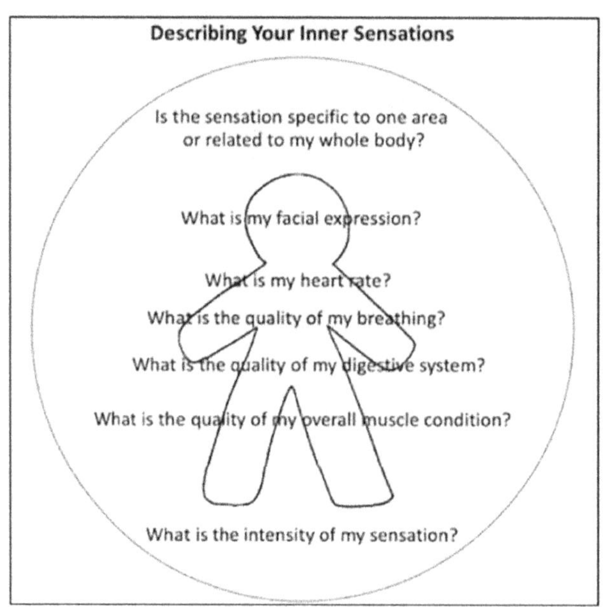

Focus	Sample Descriptors
Facial Expression	smiling, frowning, clenched jaw, relaxed jaw, flaring nostrils
Heart Rate	fast, slow, quiet, loud
Breathing Characteristics	easy, difficult, breathless, slow, rapid
Digestive System	relaxed, quiet, noisy, blocked, nauseous, full, empty, gnawing
Muscle Condition	loose, tight, shaky, achy, trembling, twitching, fluttering
Body Temperature	comfortable, cool, frozen, numb, hot, steaming, burning
Intensity of Sensation	sharp, dull, intense, weak, soft, hard, pressure
Whole Body Descriptors	faint, tingling, vibrating

Now it's Your Turn

The purpose of this exercise is to develop or enhance your capacity to connect to your inner sensations. You may be already well attuned to the clues your body provides throughout your day. If so, this exercise will allow you to articulate your unique cues and patterns. However, suppose you are like me, beginning with little appreciation of how your body speaks to you. In that case, this exercise will set a foundation that you can revisit and build on while learning the unique language of your inner bodily sensations.

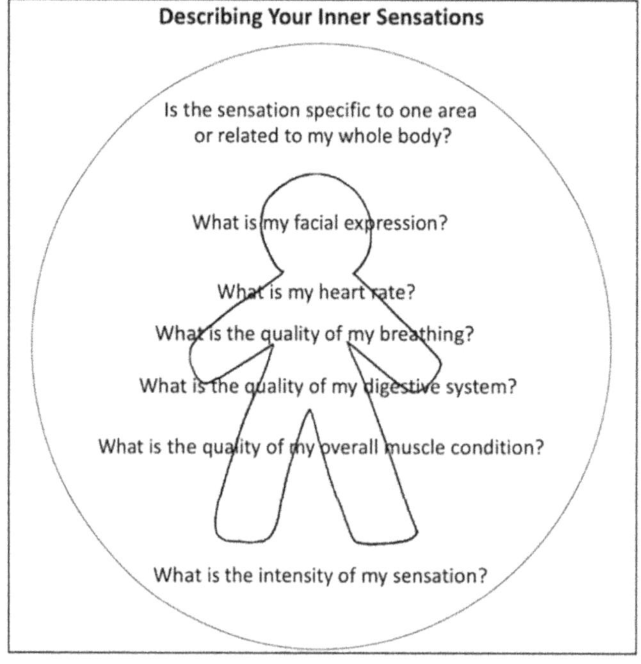

Guidepost 2: Describing the Role of Feelings

Simply stated, feelings[1] arise when you interpret bodily sensations through your mind. For example, when you smile, your heart rate might quiet, your breathing might slow down, and your muscles might relax. Not surprisingly, your mind interprets this internal state as feeling happy. On the other hand, when you frown, your heart might beat faster, you could have trouble drawing a full breath, you may become a bit nauseous, your muscles might become shaky, you may be on the verge of tears. This internal state is interpreted as feeling sad.

---

[1] Feelings and emotions are described as separate concepts in that emotions tend to be manifested subconsciously whereas feelings are always conscious and therefore directly accessible (Damasio, 2018, p. 102). Consequently, in this workbook I have chosen to use the word feelings as opposed to emotions. However, it is important to note that this distinction is not applied consistently throughout the literature. At times, you will find emotions and feelings used interchangeably.

Why is making this connection between inner sensations and feelings so important?

Your inner or physical sensations often occur well below the level of your consciousness. Feelings are words that describe your inner state. So, to further refine your capacity for self-awareness, it is helpful to look to your bodily sensations for cues and then connect these to a single or multiple descriptors of feelings.

To help make this connection, the chart below shows 8 basic feelings expanded and refined with further descriptors (Mellody, 2003). Capacity for self-awareness is strengthened when you can identify which feelings best resonate with your inner sensation(s). The following exercise is designed to help you make this connection.

8 Basic Feelings			
FEAR	Scared Anxious Threatened Rejected Insecure	**LOVE**	Affection Tenderness Compassion Passion Desire
ANGER	Mad Hurt Resentful Frustrated	**SURPRISE**	Confused Startled Amazed
SAD	Guilty Despair Lonely Bored	**HAPPY**	Content Joy Proud Optimistic Peaceful Hopeful Excited
SHAME	Embarrassed Humble Exposed	**GUILT**	Regretful Contrite Remorseful

Now it's Your Turn

You probably have a conventional response when someone asks, *How Are You Feeling?* Mine is *Fine, thanks. How are you?* This exercise invites you to consider a different way of responding by inviting you to drop into your inner landscape and choose a descriptor or two that best reflects your bodily sensations. It takes practice to make your body-mind connection. Over time, you will discover common patterns, and it will become second nature for you to fully appreciate your feelings.

Connecting to Your Feelings

- Choose a feeling, and then bring to mind a particular situation when it was present for you. Referring back to the descriptors in Guidepost 1, describe the bodily sensations you experienced in relation to that feeling.

- Following the example below, complete the chart on the next page.

- As you complete the chart feel free to go back and forth between bodily sensations and feelings. It may take a few iterations before the connection becomes clear for you. Also, with each iteration you may discover more nuances and gain a greater understanding of how feelings and bodily sensations connect in your particular system.

FEELING	BODILY SENSATIONS	COMMENTS or NOTES
Example: HAPPY	Location of sensation: overall; Facial expression: smiling; Heart Rate: steady & quiet; Breathing: easy; Digestive System: comfortably full; Muscles: relaxed; Level of Intensity: comfortable	When I am happy, my mind is quiet and fully anchored in my body.

Choose your feeling and fill in the sensations and comments or notes below:		
FEELING	**BODILY SENSATIONS**	**COMMENTS or NOTES**
	Location of sensation: Facial expression: Heart Rate: Breathing: Digestive System: Muscles: Level of Intensity:	When I am . . .
	Location of sensation: Facial expression: Heart Rate: Breathing: Digestive System: Muscles: Level of Intensity:	When I am . . .
Take a moment to comment on how easy or difficult this exercise was for you and why:		

Guidepost 3: Making the Connection to Actions

The diagram below builds on the first two guideposts and elaborates on the connection between inner sensations and feelings. As a reminder, feelings arise when the mind interprets bodily sensations. This combination creates the mind/body connection. Within this third guidepost, you will complete the cycle by learning how inner sensations and feelings work together to influence your actions.

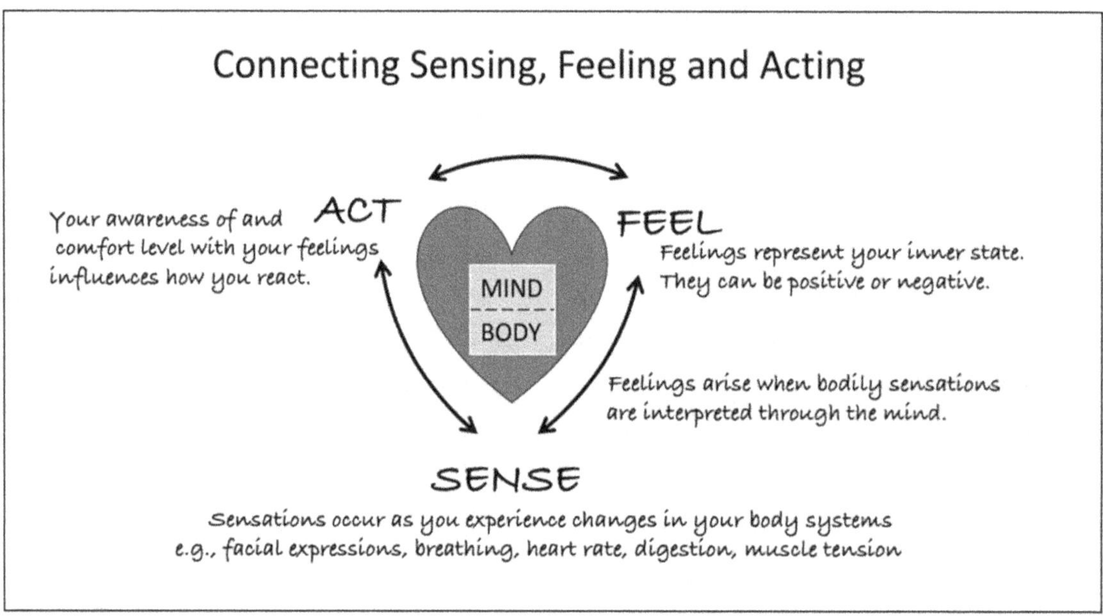

For example, if you experience an increased heart rate, your mind could interpret this sensation as fear. As a result, your leg muscles may tense as you prepare to run. This is only one possible interpretation. Alternatively, the increase in your heart rate as you sit next to someone is translated as feeling love and desire. If that is the case, your action might be to move a bit closer.

In this fashion, your actions become the outward manifestation of your inner sensations and feelings. Importantly, as explained in the following paragraph, developing self-awareness also allows you to consciously choose actions that restore, maintain, or enhance your well-being.

As indicated in the above diagram, feelings are either described as being positive or negative. A negative feeling is often experienced as being unpleasant or uncomfortable. This unpleasant sensation usually stems from an inner biological system that is out of balance and often in an unhealthy state. The more out of balance or unhealthy your system, the greater the level of discomfort you experience. Alternatively, describing a positive feeling as pleasant corresponds to an inner system that is in balance and supporting good health. Consequently, using self-awareness, you can consciously choose actions that support the good health.

Now it's Your Turn

Developing self-awareness requires paying attention to the intricate connection between your bodily sensations, feelings, and actions. With experience, seeing how the connection plays out for you will become second nature. The following exercise provides a starting point.

Making the Connection to Actions

This is a free writing exercise.
Start by setting aside 10 minutes and finding a quiet spot to complete the exercise.
As you become familiar with the process,
you will find that paying attention to the connection between your
bodily sensations, feelings, and actions will become a natural part of your day.

- Think about something you did over the past week. It can be something that stood out for you or something you undertake on a routine basis. In no particular order, list your bodily sensations, feelings, and what you were doing in that moment. Be careful not to overthink this exercise and keep it simple.

- As you review what you have written, see if you can describe how your inner sensations and feelings influenced your actions.

Guidepost 4: Experiencing Your Inner Shift

An Inner Shift happens when your actions fully align with your feelings and sensations. This moment is often accompanied by a sensation of release as your muscles relax. You spontaneously take a deep breath as your body lets go of any held tension. You sit up a bit straighter. There is a lightness to your step. In that moment, your iGPS is fully on-line. You have robust information regarding the condition of your inner landscape, paving the way for full access to your Inner Wisdom. As your mind and body connect, you know with full certainty that you are navigating your path fully in accordance with your heart's desire. However, experiencing an Inner Shift can be very subtle since:

- Acting does not necessarily imply you are doing anything overt or visible. For example, you could choose to simply sit still as you take some time to plan your next action;
- The connections between sensing, feeling, and acting are far from linear, and so it is hard to predict exactly when you might experience an Inner Shift;
- The sensations accompanying an Inner Shift can be quite fleeting and transient, and
- You are constantly exposed to situations that influence your capacity to experience, let alone maintain, the alignment required to experience an Inner Shift.

These situations are referred to as *prompts*[2]. As captured on the lower left-hand lower quadrant of the diagram below, prompts include:

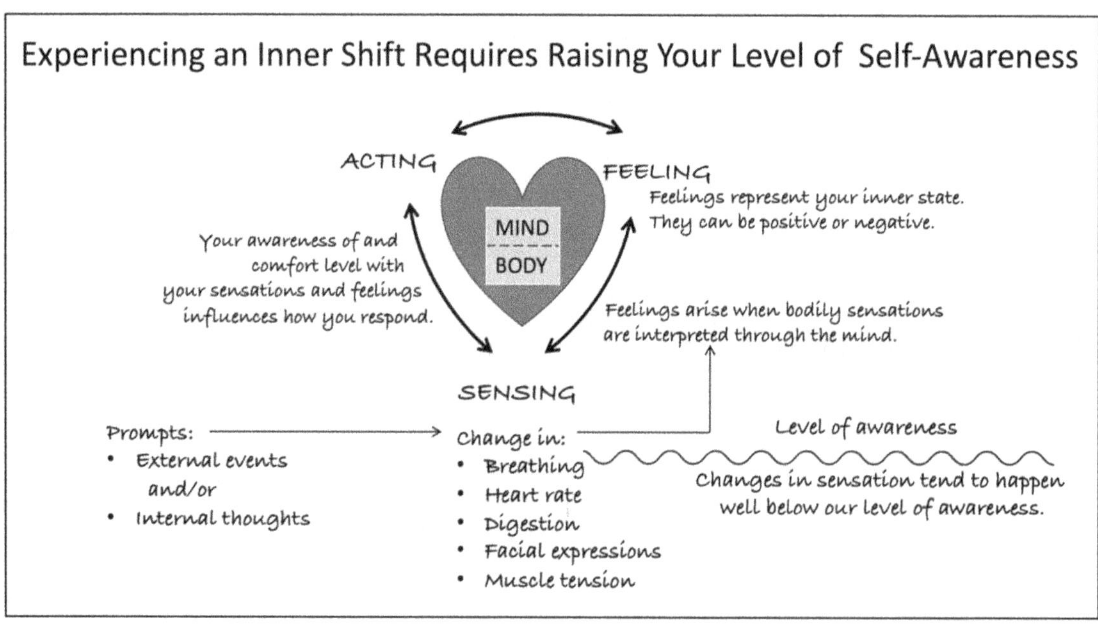

---

[2] The word trigger is commonly used to describe an event that may provoke a change in sensation. However, the word trigger refers to a unique circumstance where exposure to a situation causes someone to revisit a particularly traumatic event often resulting in a person becoming extremely overwhelmed or distressed. This condition is captured in the term *Post Traumatic Stress Disorder*. This level of response is best dealt with in cooperation with a trained mental health professional.
 • An event in your external environment, and/or
 • Your internally generated thoughts.

Exposure to these prompts can throw you out of balance as you experience a change in bodily sensations and feelings. The challenge is for you to re-act in a way that re-establishes balance or alignment. To maintain or re-experience your Inner Shift.

As illustrated in the right-hand lower quadrant of the diagram, and as explained in Guideposts 1 and 2, these changes in sensation often happen well below our level of awareness. This is a good thing because it means we can trust our body to *self-regulate*—to keep us healthy by quietly operating in the background as we encounter different prompts. However, a change in sensation may mean that you have encountered a situation that is taking you off your desired path. Consequently, it is important to develop awareness of these moments or what I like to refer to *as raising the wavy line.*

Consciously monitoring your internal world by practicing Self-awareness provides information to your iGPS regarding the condition of your inner landscape. You know the extent to which your sensations, feelings, and actions are out of balance or misaligned. With this knowledge in hand, you can determine whatever action is required to course correct so you can stay on your chosen path. As you take the action that is right for you, your system comes back into balance. With a sigh of relief once again you experience your Inner Shift and know that you are back on chosen your path.

Now it's Your Turn

The purpose of this exercise is for you to become familiar with the two different kinds of prompts and how they influence your capacity to maintain or experience an Inner Shift. This is a sophisticated skill. Have patience with yourself as you uncover your unique patterns, what you need to do to create alignment, and become familiar with how you personally experience an Inner Shift.

Experiencing Your Inner Shift

Describe a prompt you encountered that was not aligned with your Heart's Desire. Consider either:

- An external event that had an impact on you, or
- An internal thought that was not in keeping with your desired direction.

Describe your reaction to this prompt,
including any change in bodily sensations and/or feelings that arose.

Describe how you responded and what actions you took.

Finally, reflect on the impact of your actions.

- Did your actions bring you back to your desired path?

- Were you able to experience an inner shift? If so, describe your experience.

In Summary

The focus of this chapter was building your capacity for self-awareness. The importance of developing self-awareness and the challenge of doing it well cannot be underestimated. It is a life-long journey and critical to ensuring that your actions keep you on your chosen path. However, no matter how self-aware you have become, you will no doubt encounter unexpected bumps in the road. These may be small or large bumps but regardless of size they will challenge your ability to remain balanced and stay on your path. By introducing the quality of self-compassion, Chapter 6 will help you learn how to navigate these bumps with ease.

Insights and Questions

Use this space to capture anything that may have surprised you
as you completed this chapter or
something you may be wondering about as you move into Chapter 6.

Key Concepts

Inner Geographical Positioning System (iGPS)
Assists in knowing where you are at all times, assessing the extent to which your inner landscape is in positioned to support your ongoing journey. Your iGPS paves the way for full access to your Inner Wisdom and therefore helps to guide you in the right direction.

Inner Shift
A sensation of release experienced as you let go of any held tension. This sensation can be accompanied by spontaneous engagement in deep breathing as your muscles relax. You may also experience a feeling of lightness.

Prompts
Any event that poses a threat to your ability to maintain your inner balance.

Self-Awareness
Self-awareness is the ability to monitor your inner world – knowing the relationship between your thoughts, feelings, and reactions (Goleman,2020, p.269).

References

Damasio A. (2018). The Strange Order of Things. Life, Feeling, and the Making of Cultures. New York, NY: Pantheon Books.

Goleman D. (2020). Emotional Intelligence. Why It Can Matter More than IQ. 25th Anniversary Edition. New York, NY: Bantam Books.

Goleman D. (1998). The emotional intelligence of leaders. Leader to Leader, September (10), p. 20-26.

Mellody P. (2003). Facing Codependence: What It Is, Where It Comes From, How It Sabotages Our Lives. New York, NY: HarperCollins Publishers.

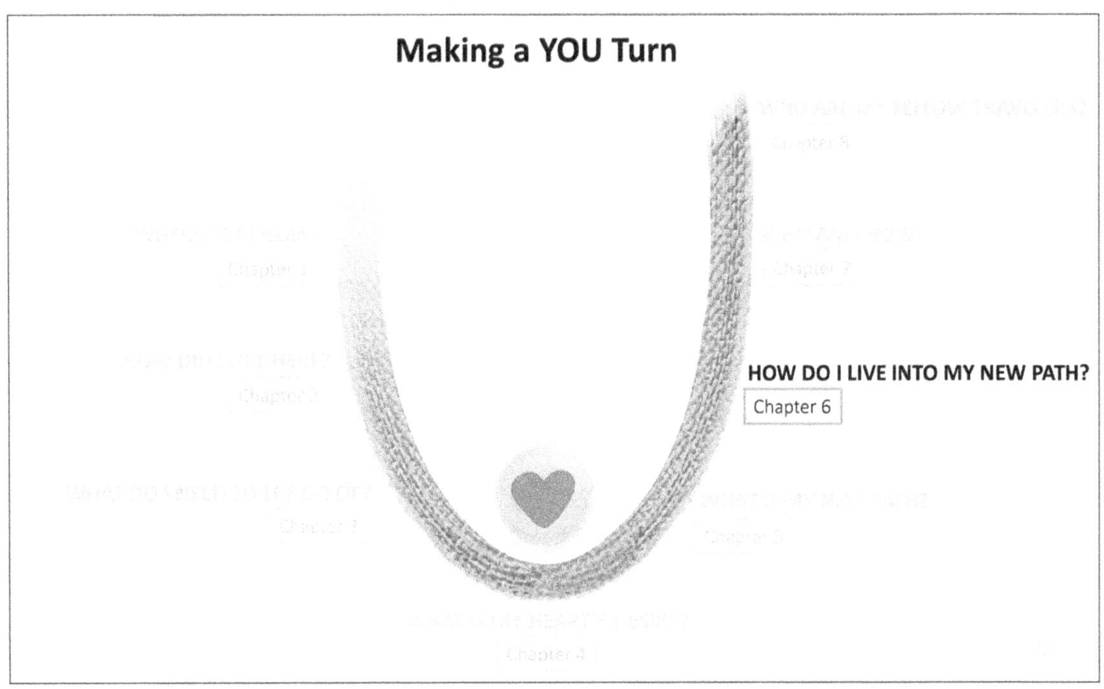

Chapter 6

How Do I Live into My New Path?

Drawing on Self-Compassion as Your Guiding Compass

Chapter 5 focused on building your capacity for self-awareness. Self-awareness tells you when your actions
fully align with your heart's desire. It becomes your
inner geographical positioning system—your iGPS, helping you to stay on your chosen path.

However, there will be times when you encounter challenges despite your best intentions. Perhaps
something did not go quite as you had hoped, or someone says or does something that takes you by
surprise. In these moments, you may find yourself struggling to stay on course.

In this chapter, you will continue to enhance your capacity for self-awareness
and explore further what happens for you in these moments.
This deeper understanding will help you identify when and how to engage in self-compassion,
or what I have come to know as the energy of love.

My Invitation to You

The story below describes what happened when I encountered an unexpected conversation;
one that, in the past, I might have struggled with staying calm and engaged.
But instead, I was able to stay present in the moment.

As you read my story, reflect on the following:

- Describe a similar situation which presented a challenge or where you struggled to stay calm and focused.

- How did you respond?

Staying on the Path:
Tapping into the Energy of Love

It is a Sunday night in January 2021. My ex and I are having dinner together at my house. In the middle of our conversation, he tells me he wants to share what drove him to drink. Hesitating, he then looks at me as if to say, "Maybe it's better that I keep this to myself." I pause and wonder how I feel about his potential revelation. In the past, I may have felt threatened and left the table angry. Alternatively, I might have checked out and simply stopped listening. Instead, I find myself sitting calmly in my chair, ready to listen and intensely curious. Extending an invitation, I say, "It's okay, go ahead; I am more than ready to listen." It has taken me the better part of two years to get to this point.

Following my return from Italy in 2018, we rarely saw each other. I could not live with the uncertainty and ongoing disappointment of his relapses. My anger was palpable. I needed space and distance from the situation. However, I was worried that my anger was turning into chronic bitterness. I did not want to live the rest of my life this way. So, I started seeing a therapist to help me through this difficult time. One session in particular stands out for me.

My therapist's office is long and narrow. As I enter, to the left are two chairs and a couch. This is where our sessions typically take place: my therapist in a chair, a pad of paper and pen in hand, and me poised on the edge of the couch. To the right is a table. It is the size of a massage table with a black cushioned cover.

I didn't even notice the table when I first started seeing her. I always went immediately to the couch to begin telling the latest version of my story. But on this day, she tells me, "It's time to go to the table." A bit desperately, I immediately think about what purpose the table has. I need to know. That will really help me. Why I don't ask, I do not know, but I have plenty of reason to trust her. She has only shown me unconditional acceptance and love, and her office is a safe space for me to share my innermost thoughts, worries, and desires.

When I reach the table, she has me lie down on my back while she ever so gently moves my legs and arms back and forth. Eventually, she says, "What's coming up for you? What do you feel? Where do you feel it?" I become acutely aware of a knot at the top of my stomach that radiates into my throat. My breathing is shallow, and I have very little connection to the rest of my body. She continues to move my arms and legs softly. As I begin to relax, the tension in my stomach releases. I become aware of a soft tingling sensation in my arms and legs—as if the released energy from the knot is now flowing into the rest of my body. My chest expands, and I begin breathing much more deeply. At that moment, I feel completely relaxed, safe, and secure.

Leaving the session, I know something significant has taken place. As a scientist, I take a deep dive into better understanding my experience. I wanted to know how I could go from being so tense and uptight one moment to a relaxed, calm state the next. Through this research and practice, I become skilled in reading the signals from my body and finding strategies that help me shift into a relaxed, open stance when I begin to struggle. These skills have become an effective way of acknowledging but not being driven by the challenges that come my way. I think of these moments as opportunities to consciously shift from the energy of fear into the energy of love.

My hard work pays off. As I wait to hear what my ex has to say, I no longer feel anger or bitterness. I stay relaxed and present, open to what he wants to tell me about what drove him to drinking. Responding to my invitation to continue, he explains that he was lonely in our marriage. He further explains that his loneliness became his trigger to drink. Knowing other aspects of his story, I sense that his loneliness runs very deep and started long before we met. I realize that this is his story, and all I'm required to do is listen.

This is my new way of showing up—being able to stay present in a conversation without getting caught up in a particular story or outcome.

For me, this is what it is like to live through the energy of love.

Lessons Learned

By definition, a new path contains unfamiliar territory. No one is perfect. Despite your best intentions, falling back into old ways and habitual patterns is easy. This is particularly true when you are on a transformative journey—one where you are consciously adopting new beliefs and ways of living.

As described in my story, an essential part of my transformation was to embody a new way of showing up. But this did not come naturally to me. I had spent so much time in a disconnected, contracted state that being present as calm, relaxed, and open-hearted was a new experience. And yet, once I encountered this way of being, there was no turning back. I had to learn how to use this new fuel, or what I came to think of as the *energy of love*, to support my ongoing YOU Turn.

Intriguingly, I found embracing self-compassion a necessary foundation for living through the energy of love. Surprisingly, I learned that just by virtue of being human, self-compassion is always readily accessible. However, I also learned that it takes some skill to tap into, let alone maintain, such a kind, open-hearted presence.

Accordingly, the guideposts for this chapter are as follows:

1. Building a foundation for self-compassion;
2. Learning to pause and assess;
3. Finding glimmers;
4. Embracing self-compassion.

Refresher:
Creating Safety

In Guidepost #1 in Chapter 4, you learned the importance of
feeling safe and at ease in order to connect to your heart's desire.
Feeling safe is also a necessary condition for drawing on self-compassion.

Take a minute to revisit the conditions that make you feel safe and at ease.

- What physical spaces invite stillness?
- What sounds, smells, and sights bring you comfort? For example, music or nature.
- When have you felt completely at ease? Describe this moment.

Throughout this chapter, call on these conditions to support your journey into self-compassion.

Guidepost 1: Building a Foundation for Self-Compassion

You know you are drawing on self-compassion when you respond to your struggles and imperfections with the same warmth and kindness you would extend to a good friend or loved one. Reacting with kindness requires entering into or maintaining a calm disposition when faced with a challenging situation. This guidepost explains how recognizing the unique features of your body chemistry or *physiological states* is a foundational skill for accessing a calm state and embracing self-compassion.

As illustrated in the diagram below, three possible states are available when encountering different situations: calm, mobilized, or immobilized. Each state has a unique impact on a particular body system.

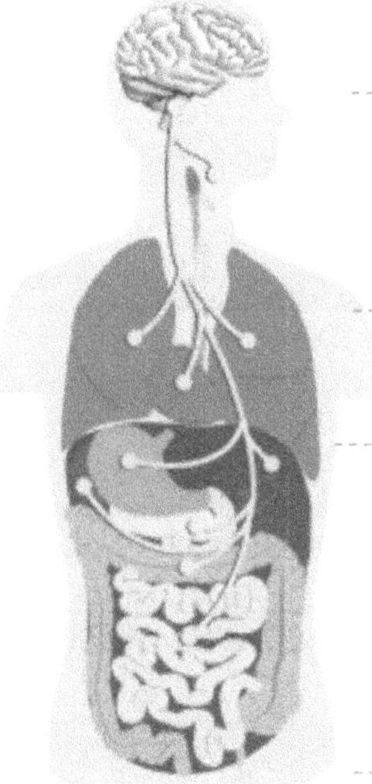

You are in a calm state when life is going well. Your environment is safe, and you can easily connect to yourself and others. Accordingly, your facial features are relaxed, and you smile often. Also, your speech and tone speed are easy and not strained or harsh.

However, if you judge a situation as threatening, you enter a state of mobilization. Your heart and respiration rate increase to support the burst of energy needed to fight or flee; however, the situation does not necessarily have to be a direct physical threat. For example, a friend or colleague might be expressing an opinion you disagree with, causing you to become activated. Or when life feels overwhelming, you might react by attacking or wanting to escape (Dana, 2021).

When conditions decline significantly, you may experience immobilization and quite literally become frozen to the spot. This state is connected to your digestive system which slows right down as you become drained of energy. Experiencing a threat on your life is an extreme example of a situation that induces immobilization. In a less extreme, everyday example, you may enter this state when feeling trapped in an ongoing cycle of endless challenges or when losing hope that a difficult situation can change.

Now it's Your Turn

Like a guard dog, your nervous system is constantly scanning your surroundings for cues of safety and danger and responding accordingly (Porges, 2017). Quite often, this dynamic happens well below your level of awareness. However, with practice you may recognize your unique experience of these inner states. Keep in mind that the descriptions provided above are general guidelines. It may take some time to gain knowledge of your experience of the three states. Feel free to come back to this exercise whenever you discover a new insight.

Building Your Foundation for Self-Compassion

Use the chart below to describe a situation
when you experienced a particular state and how you responded.

State:
Situation: Event and/or conditions under which you experienced this state.
Responses: How you reacted including any physical sensations.

State #1: Calm: Safe and Connected
Situation:

Your Response:

State #2: Mobilized: Fight or Flight
Situation:

Your Response:

State #3: Immobilized: Freeze
Situation:

Your Response:

Guidepost 2: Learning to Pause and Assess

Throughout the day, your nervous system is constantly shifting between states. These shifts may be small and subtle or significant and distinct. Depending on past experiences, you have developed a pattern that is unique to you. For example, there may be specific situations where you become mobilized and react accordingly—fight or flight. Alternatively, you may find circumstances when you don't have the capacity to respond and become immobile—freezing in place.

Over time, your responses become second nature to you. In fact, when facing a threat, everyone has a preferred reaction to either mobilize: fight or take flight, or immobilize: freeze into position. This is referred to as your default state or *home away from home* (Dana, 2020). However, since embracing self-compassion relies on accessing a calm foundation, you need to be aware of your shifting states, including if your preferred *home away from home* is to become mobilized—to fight or take flight, or immobilized—to freeze. You can accomplish this awareness by simply *pausing and assessing* the shifts you experience throughout the day. The following exercise is designed to guide you in this process.

Now it's Your Turn

If you are like me, you can often go about your day moving from one activity to the other without pausing, let alone assessing your state at that moment. This exercise asks you to check in and note of how your states play out during your day. It is important that you don't judge your states as being good or bad. Simply see what emerges for you.

Learning to Pause and Assess

Keep this chart close to you as you go about your day. Three times a day, at the end of the morning, afternoon, and evening pause and take a moment to place an X on the chart to indicate your state. If you find yourself experiencing more than one state in each period, feel free to use more than one X.

State (y-axis): Calm, Mobilized, Immobilized

Time of Day (x-axis): Morning, Afternoon, Evening

- Draw a line between the X's. Does this pattern look familiar to you?
- As you review your experiences, name your default state.

Guidepost 3: Finding Glimmers

Traditionally, interventions such as adopting a consistent meditation practice or mindfulness-based stress reduction have been described as the path to engaging in self-compassion. However, recent advances in neuroscience have revealed that these practices work because they promote a body chemistry that induces a calm state rather than because they still your thoughts (Porges, 2017). Using *glimmers* is a simple and effective strategy for finding your way into such a state.

A glimmer is a moment that sets you at ease or makes you smile (Dana, 2020). For example, when I become activated, a quick glance out a window calms my system . Other examples of glimmers are:

- Seeing a friendly face;
- Sitting with a favourite pet;
- Looking at a vase of flowers;
- Listening to a favourite piece of music.

The moment I experience a glimmer, I begin to breathe with more ease, my face relaxes, and my voice slows and softens. In many circumstances, all it takes is a micro-moment. Entering such a calm state can happen in the blink of an eye.

Now it's Your Turn

The purpose of this exercise is to help you identify and experience your unique glimmers. Basically, anything that is enjoyable in your environment serves as a glimmer. The challenge is to become familiar with the circumstances that help your system enter a calm state.

Finding Glimmers

You typically experience several different glimmers throughout the day. In the beginning, you may just find one glimmer. But as time goes on and you become more expert at identifying these moments, you will be surprised at how many glimmers you naturally experience during the course of a day.

- Identify a moment during your day when you experience a calm state;
- Place your hand over your heart and say the word *glimmer*;
- Pause and deepen into the experience;
- Describe the details of the glimmer and how you know you are moving into a calm state. For example, your facial muscles begin to relax. Or you start smiling. Perhaps you experience a release of tension.

Guidepost 4: Embracing Self-Compassion

You have learned the following in the first three guideposts in this chapter:

- Why achieving a calm state is foundational for experiencing self-compassion;
- The importance of pausing to assess your state and
- Using glimmers as a strategy for moving into a calm state.

Over time, taking a moment to pause and assess will simply become part of how you operate. As you become familiar with the rhythm of your body, it will become easier to access and maintain a calm state.

However, it is essential to understand that becoming increasingly calm and grounded does not mean your challenges will disappear or even decrease. Instead, you will begin to appreciate that experiencing imperfections and struggles is what makes us human. With this newfound understanding, you will naturally find ways to treat yourself with warmth and kindness, particularly when facing moments of difficulty.

This is what it means to use self-compassion as your guiding compass.

This is what it takes to live through the energy of love.

Now it's Your Turn

When you are in a calm state, you are readily able to assess what next steps you need to stay on course. Perhaps you need to spend some time alone, just breathing or walking in nature. Or, maybe it's listening to music, taking a hot bath, or connecting with friends... Only you know what strategies work best to optimize your ongoing well-being.

Embracing Self-Compassion

Embracing self-compassion means responding to your individual struggles and imperfections like you would react to a good friend or loved one with warmth and kindness.

- What strategies do you use to help a friend who is struggling?

- What strategies do you use to treat yourself with warmth and kindness?

Summary

In this chapter, you learned that treating yourself with warmth and kindness or self-compassion requires engaging in a calm disposition. Remembering moments that set you at ease or make you smile—also known as *glimmers*—was introduced as an effective strategy to help you access and maintain a calm state. In this state, being kind to yourself becomes second nature. When facing bumps in the road, self-compassion becomes your guiding compass, always keeping you on your chosen path.

You are now well on your way to making a YOU Turn. This is a long journey full of different experiences, and Chapter 7 will provide you with the opportunity to look back, reflect on, and most importantly, celebrate how far you have come.

Embracing Self-Compassion

Embracing self-compassion means responding to your individual struggles and imperfections like you would react to a good friend or loved one with warmth and kindness.

- What strategies do you use to help a friend who is struggling?

- What strategies do you use to treat yourself with warmth and kindness?

Key Concepts

Glimmer
A positive moment that sets you at ease such as seeing a friendly face, hearing a soothing sound, or noticing something enjoyable in your environment (Dana, 2020, p. 109).

Self-compassion
The act of reaching in to be with our own suffering with kindness (Dana, 2018, p.27).

References

Dana D. (2018). The Polyvagal Theory in Therapy. Engaging the Rhythm of Regulation. New York, NY: W.W. Norton & Company Inc.

Dana D. (2020). Polyvagal Exercises for Safety and Connection. 50 Client-centered Practices. New York, NY: Norton & Company Inc.

Porges S.W. (2017). The Pocket Guide to the Polyvagal Theory. The Transformative Power of Feeling Safe. NewYork, NY: Norton & Company Inc.

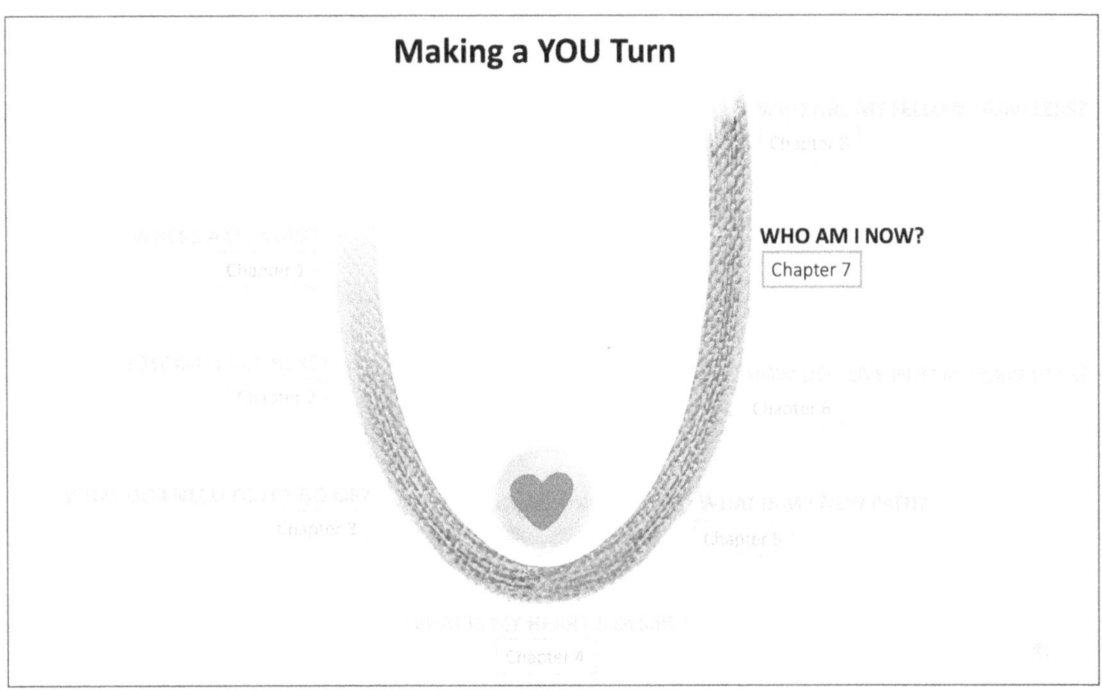

Chapter 7

Who Am I Now?

Finding Your Way Home Through Self-Acceptance

By focusing on self-awareness and self-compassion, Chapters 5 and 6 provided key strategies for staying present in the moment. Over time, practicing these skills will reinforce your inner shift away from doing what you think is expected of you into being exactly who you are.

This is what I describe as living through the essence of your presence.

In this state of self-connection, your Inner Wisdom is ever-present,
guiding you through every step along your path.

This new way of being is a significant transformation. Like a butterfly emerging from a cocoon, you will look, feel, and move very differently. Chapter 7 is all about learning how to stay on your chosen path and celebrating your new way of being present in the world.

My Invitation to You

The story below describes how I responded to an experience
of significant doubt and uncertainty as I navigated my YOU Turn.

As you read my story, reflect on the following:

- How do you relate to my experience of doubt and uncertainty?
  For example, are you surprised or . . .

- Describe any experiences of doubt and uncertainty you have encountered during your
  journey.

- How did you respond to them?

Learning To Travel With Ease:
My Journey Continues

It is the Fall of 2023. I am ready to start Chapter 5 of my workbook. My fingers are poised eagerly over the keyboard. I am so ready to dive into the details of my transformation. How much I have changed. How much lighter I feel.

My lightness is amplified by my new surroundings. It has been an eventful year.

A few months earlier, I moved into a new house. Packing up the home my family and I lived in for 23 years was a daunting task. Every cupboard, every drawer, every closet held so many memories. Being immersed in my writing helped me see these experiences in a new light. That part of my journey now feels complete. Fittingly, it is time to move on.

I sit at my desk in my new house. The sight of the fall trees create a stunning vista through the huge windows framing my writing space. As I bask in the beauty of the autumn colours, everything feels like it is falling into place. I am proud of how far I have come. Ready to shed the past, I am eager to write about my next chapter. Taking a deep breath, I sit up straight, excited to be putting my personal transformation into words.

And then something strange happens.

Staring at the computer screen, I find myself becoming overwhelmed with doubt and uncertainty. A part of me wants to write something inspirational— to describe the rewards of working so hard and how the first four chapters have paved the way for a smooth and easy path ahead. However, another part of me is acutely aware that this is untrue.

In fact, this in-depth exploration into finding myself has rendered me much more sensitive to the ups and downs of my journey. No longer able to ignore my feelings, I now fully experience times of sadness and regret. In these moments, I wonder if this is really how things are supposed to be. Life was much easier in many ways when I was out of touch with my feelings as I skated along the surface, pretending all was fine.

I sink into my chair, and I notice my shoulders are drooping. In the past, I would have made something up that sounded good on the surface. But I cannot do this now. This is not the time to start telling stories just to get it done. I want to continue writing my truth. My wheels are spinning, and I am stuck for words. Unsure of my next steps, I get up from my chair and exit my light-filled room.

The following few weeks were difficult, but I have learned to trust my Inner Wisdom. I stop fussing about my writing and continue to settle into my new house, confident that a way forward will emerge. It gradually dawns on me that I am once again in the middle of a dilemma. Perhaps it is time to follow my own advice.

So, I go back to Chapter 1 and ask myself what beliefs I hold on to that feed into my struggle. Little by little, I realize that I expected the way ahead would be smooth and easy once I found my heart's desire. I believed that the difficulties of the past would simply fall away, and I would always know the right path to take. I chuckle as I appreciate my ongoing capacity for magical thinking. My truth becomes clear.

Going with ease does not mean life will always be easy.

Indeed, living with ease means feeling every bump in the road and responding with self-awareness and self-compassion. I laugh because this is a huge change for me. Instead of taking a bypass by distracting myself when life gets hard, I can remain fully present— particularly in moments of uncertainty. Facing my challenges head-on is exactly what it takes to stay true to my heart's desire. I now know this is the transformation I must write about.

As I settle back into my new writing space, I have never felt more at home.

Lessons Learned

Completing an in-depth exploration into finding and loving yourself is a significant undertaking. It is also an ongoing journey. No matter how deep you go, you will continue to encounter new and challenging situations. Despite all your hard work, there will still be times when you somehow lose connection with your Inner Wisdom.

Therefore, in light of your experiences, it is essential to ask yourself, *Who am I Now?* This will enable you to fully appreciate how much you have changed. It will also help you to stay connected to your Inner Wisdom and when required, reconnect with it as you fully see, accept, and celebrate how far you have traveled.

Accordingly, the guideposts for Chapter 7 are as follows:

- Tracking your transformation;
- Staying connected to your Inner Wisdom;
- Deepening your journey;
- Arriving home through self-acceptance.

Refresher:
Revisiting the Continuum of Self-Connection

In Chapter 2, you encountered the Continuum of Self-Connection
as a way of charting the direction of your journey. Then, in Chapter 4 you used this continuum
to map your progression in making your YOU Turn.

The Continuum of Self Connection

YOU ARE:
- Driven by external rewards & recognition
- Focused on thinking & reasoning
- Not able to recognize or express feelings
- Not aware of internal sensations or cues
- Not able to describe personal needs

DRIVING FORCES:

Past Experiences
- Exposure to Big T and/or little t trauma(s)
- Family history

Cultural & Social Context

YOU ARE:
- Readily able to access & act from Inner Wisdom
- Able to fully integrate mind & body
- Comfortable expressing a full range of feelings
- Highly aware of personal needs
- Have the capacity to balance your needs with the needs of others

DISCONNECTED

IN YOUR LIFE:
- On the surface all appears to be fine
- Unacknowledged tensions exist deep below
- Life is chaotic, confusing & unpredictable particularly in the face of unexpected challenges

CONNECTED

IN YOUR LIFE:
- There is clear alignment between your inner & outer world
- Nothing is hidden
- You go with ease even in the face of unexpected challenges

Before you start Chapter 7, take a moment to reflect on your journey along this continuum.

Guidepost 1: Tracking Your Transformation

As you travel along the YOU Turn, you will experience significant *aha* moments. New portals will open within those moments, and as you step over the threshold, you will realize that you will never see or experience life the same way. For example, when I learned early on that the only way forward was for me to change, I never again saw a situation or another person needing fixing.

However, as described in Chapter 1, transformative change can also happen gradually. As explained in Chapter 5, developing the required capacity for self-awareness is subtle and nuanced. Consequently, as expressed in my story, I easily lost track of how far I had travelled—how much I had changed. This lack of awareness made me susceptible to experiencing doubt and uncertainty.

To get back on track, I found using the Continuum of Self-Connection as a reference point helpful. However, unlike in Chapter 4, the task this time was not about taking a tally of milestones achieved but instead focusing on my expanding capacity for self-awareness. I wanted to know if I was showing up differently and how I had changed.

To get answers, I started considering how I felt at the beginning of my journey, and as I reviewed the list, the one word, *closed*, captured an accurate description of how I was showing up. I was in a highly reactive state, closed to any possibility that I needed to change.

This starkly contrasted with how I was showing up in the present moment.

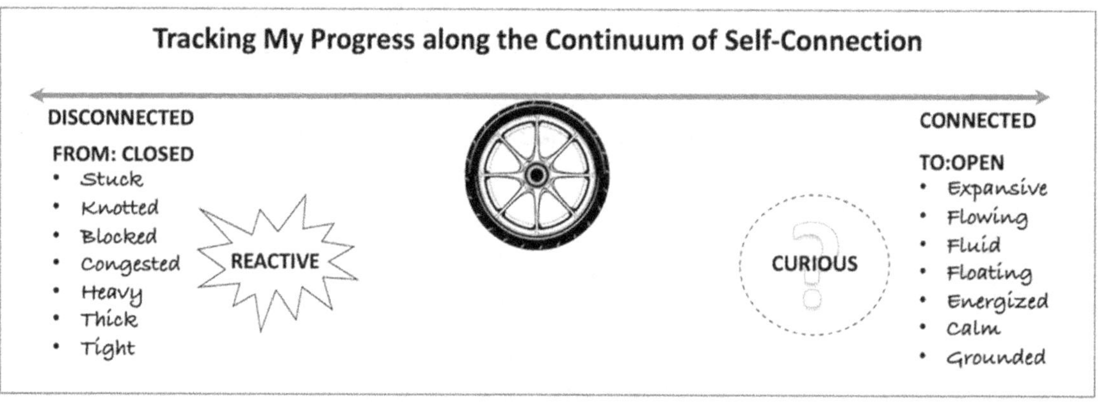

After this realization, *open* became the word I used to describe myself. The most significant change was that I could respond to new situations with curiosity, deliberately taking the time I needed to consider my next steps. In difficult situations, I might still experience reactivity, but I could now pause and calmly consider my next steps rather than move immediately to action.

This exercise of looking in my rear-view mirror reinforced that I was indeed showing up very differently because of my YOU Turn experience. The following exercise will allow you to answer the question, *How have you changed over the course of this journey?*

Now it's your turn

As you make a YOU Turn, the changes you experience are unique to you. Some of these changes may be obvious, yet some may be more subtle. The following exercise is designed to help you put words to your experience. This is an important milestone in your journey, so take your time. If you have difficulty describing your changes, you might find it helpful to refer back to Chapter 5—Building Capacity for Self-Awareness.

Tracking Your Transformation

Take a moment to review the Continuum of Self-Connection.

Take yourself back to the start of your journey and
list some words capturing how you were showing up.
Then, fast forward to today and list some words describing how you are showing up now.

Sometimes, these changes are hard to articulate with words. Feel free to create a drawing or choose colours that represent where you started and where you are today.

The Continuum of Self Connection

YOU ARE:
- Driven by external rewards & recognition
- Focused on thinking & reasoning
- Not able to recognize or express feelings
- Not aware of internal sensations or cues
- Not able to describe personal needs

DRIVING FORCES:

Past Experiences
- Exposure to Big T and/or little t trauma(s)
- Family history

Cultural & Social Context

YOU ARE:
- Readily able to access & act from Inner Wisdom
- Able to fully integrate mind & body
- Comfortable expressing a full range of feelings
- Highly aware of personal needs
- Have the capacity to balance your needs with the needs of others

DISCONNECTED

CONNECTED

IN YOUR LIFE:
- On the surface all appears to be fine
- Unacknowledged tensions exist deep below
- Life is chaotic, confusing & unpredictable particularly in the face of unexpected challenges

IN YOUR LIFE:
- There is clear alignment between your inner & outer world
- Nothing is hidden
- You go with ease even in the face of unexpected challenges

FROM:
Describe how you were showing up
as you started your journey:

TO:
Describe how you are showing up
at this point in your journey:

Guidepost 2: Staying Connected to Your Inner Wisdom

Taking the time to track my progress reminded me that a YOU Turn is not a one-way journey. I discovered that I could still experience feelings of disconnection—doubt and uncertainty—depending on the circumstance. I saw this struggle as an indicator that I had lost connection to my Inner Wisdom, and my iGPS had temporarily gone offline. I also knew that I had a choice about how to respond.

Previously, when things became difficult, I had a natural tendency to avoid any pain or struggle. I was very skilled at *taking a bypass*. Like an off-ramp, a bypass allowed me to steer clear of any messiness or pain that blocked my path. My strategy was to turn to social media as a way of numbing myself from any discomfort. However, as described in the following chart, there are many different strategies for ignoring painful feelings or taking a bypass (Kelly, 2024; Plett, 2020).

Bypass Strategies	
Type	**Description**
Spiritual Bypass	Using meditation or religion to sidestep feelings of discomfort.
Cognitive Overpass	Using logic and words, reading every book on the topic, as a way of employing rationalization to rise above the issue.
Psychological Underpass	Using therapy to appear to be dealing with the messiness all the while staying below the radar and avoiding the struggle or pain.

This list is by no means exhaustive. Other diversionary tactics include turning to any soothing behaviour such as drinking, taking drugs, focusing on work, engaging in social media, etcetera. Deflecting blame onto others is also an effective avoidance strategy.

With this knowledge in my repair kit and drawing on my newfound capacity for self-compassion, I could pause and assess my situation. Consequently, despite struggling, I deliberately did not go to my preferred bypass of watching endless movies. Instead, I simply stopped writing and continued settling into my new house. As a result, I returned to a calm state and remained present, creating the space required for my Inner Wisdom to come back online.

As an aside, some bypass strategies can be very useful in providing temporary relief when you are facing a difficult situation. In that case, it may be perfectly fine for you to engage in a temporary distraction while you consider your next steps. Some of these bypass activities may provide great support and nourishment if used as a deliberate relaxation strategy. However, a bypass is counterproductive when used as a singular strategy to avoid any growth or personal development in times of difficulty.

Now it's your turn

This exercise is designed for you to become familiar with your preferred bypass strategies. It will help you identify when you are using a distraction simply as a rest stop along your journey so, when you are ready, you can continue refreshed and energized, or when you are using a bypass to avoid a struggle or dealing with a difficult situation.

Staying Connected to Your Inner Wisdom

Review the chart below. Write down any strategies you typically use when you hit a bump in the road or experience doubt and uncertainty. You may only have one, but this list is by no means exhaustive, so feel free to include anything you use as a diversionary strategy.
For each strategy, reflect on the extent to which it provides you with a healthy temporary distraction versus a way to avoid dealing with struggle or pain.

Bypass Strategies

Type	Description
• Spiritual Bypass:	Using meditation or religion to sidestep feelings of discomfort.
• Cognitive Overpass:	Using logic and words by reading every book on the topic as a way of employing rationalization to rise above the issue.
• Psychological Underpass:	Using therapy to appear to be dealing with the messiness all the while staying below the radar and avoiding the struggle or pain.
• Other diversionary tactics:	Turning to soothing behaviors such as work, social media, exercise, drugs, alcohol, sex etcetera. Deflecting blame onto others.

Reflect on your preferred bypass strategies:

Guidepost 3: Deepening Your Journey

How do you continue when your Inner Wisdom goes offline, and you are tempted to take a bypass? In these moments, it is important to remember that a YOU Turn is not a predictable, linear, stepwise journey. At any point, you can experience a dilemma that makes you wonder about your next steps. These can be major or minor events, but the result is the same. Every new dilemma you encounter provides an opportunity to embark on a deeper exploration. Doing so can be quite straightforward.

Whenever you enter unfamiliar territory, return to the beginning and, in light of your new situation, revisit the key questions found in Chapter 1. As illustrated in the following chart, returning to these questions helped me to, once again, unearth an assumption I did not realize I was holding on to—an assumption that was contributing to my doubt and uncertainty at this point in my journey.

Deepening My Journey – Returning to the Beginning

- **Where am I now?**
  I am experiencing doubt and uncertainty as I question whether or not I have really changed.
- **What is my current dilemma?**
  I am wondering if I have truly changed and why I still experience bumps in the road?
- **What assumptions are contributing to my current situation?**
  I believe that as a result of embarking on a journey of personal growth and transformation, my life will always be smooth and easy.
- **How can I shift my assumptions in a way that helps me move forward?**
  I realize and embrace the fact that I can go with ease even in the face of a struggle.

- -

My Shifting Assumption

From:		To:
As a result of undertaking a journey of personal growth, life will always be smooth and easy.	⟶	Going with ease does not mean that life will always be easy.

This exercise allowed me to clearly identify an underlying assumption about my current dilemma. At some point, I had adopted the belief that successfully undertaking this journey would mean never struggling again—life would always be smooth and easy. Revealing the fallacy of my thinking helped me to shift my assumptions yet again. I could see that I could still go with ease even in the face of a struggle. This shift enabled me to reconnect with my Inner Wisdom and further deepen my exploration of personal growth. Using the following exercise, you can learn to respond with ease in the face of new challenges.

Now it's your turn

Inevitably, you will encounter bumps along the road—times when you experience doubt and uncertainty. In these moments it may feel like you are going backward, and going back to the beginning will indeed help you create a deeper understanding of who you are currently as you continue your journey.

Deepening Your Journey

Reflect on the following questions whenever you encounter a new struggle or challenge.
Can you identify an assumption that is contributing to your struggle?
Can you shift your assumption to allow you to continue your journey calmly?

- **Where am I now?**

- **What is my current dilemma?**

- **What assumptions are contributing to my current situation?**

- **How can I shift my assumptions in a way that helps me move forward?**

My Shifting Assumption

From: ⟶   To:

Guidepost 4: Arriving Home through Self-Acceptance

The questions from Guidepost 3, over time, have become second nature to me. I am continuously surprised at what I learn while unearthing and shifting my long-held assumptions and, ultimately, how freeing it is to take action that fully aligns with my true beliefs and heart's desire. *I can now embrace myself for who I am, both my strengths and limitations.* This is the true definition of self-acceptance.

I have also learned that self-acceptance is not an end state but instead requires an ongoing process of exploration (Jeffcoat, 2013). As described in Guideposts 1 and 2, this is a process that relies heavily upon the elements of self-awareness and self-compassion. As illustrated in the diagram below, self-awareness and self-compassion support the process of self-acceptance, which provides the power or energy required to move the wheel toward self-connection.

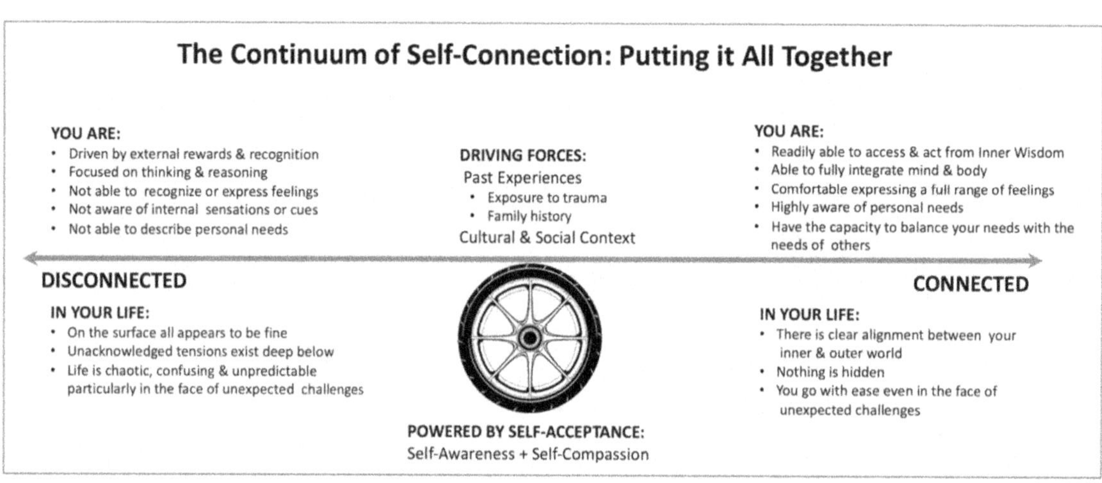

For example, when I understood how my long-held beliefs fed into my current dilemma, I felt myself relaxing into the moment. Once again, I began to experience enhanced feelings of openness and self-connection as my wheel moved to the right.

However, the diagram also illustrates the fluidity of the journey. The wheel is constantly in motion as you encounter and respond to external and internal events.

For me, the phrase, *Traveling with ease does not necessarily mean life will always be easy,* serves as a reminder that there will always be times when I experience moments of disconnection. Accordingly, I have adopted this phrase as my new mantra, reminding me that challenging times are not something to avoid but rather a valuable part of my journey. When I choose to invoke this phrase, my feet become firmly planted, I relax, almost melt, into the moment, and I am fully confident that the steps I am taking are exactly right for me.

That is also when I understand that my longing for intimacy—to be truly seen and valued for exactly who I am— was within my reach all along. I simply had to learn to see into myself.

Welcome Home!

Now it's your turn

It sounds so cliché but making a YOU Turn is truly not about where you end up but how you show up every day and every moment. After completing this chapter, you will know what has changed for you and how you are showing up differently. You will also realize that this is a lifelong journey where you continue to experience new insights and understandings. The following exercise invites you to create a new mantra to guide you as you deepen into the journey of your YOU Turn.

Arriving Home Through Self-Acceptance:
Creating Your New Mantra

Create a new mantra that captures your motivation for continuing your journey.

- To get started, write the mantra that has been guiding you to this point.

For example, as described in Chapter 1, mine was:

Find yourself; it's been too long.
Trust yourself; it will make you strong.

Or perhaps you have adopted a series of mantras along the way.
Feel free to use this space to capture any significant sayings that have guided you to this point.

- Reflect on each of your statements and consider whether they still resonate for you.

For example, my YOU Turn experience supported me to be very clear about who I am. It allowed me to love and accept every part of me. It was time to adopt my new mantra:

Going with ease does not mean that life will always be easy.

Use this space to write your new mantra.

In Summary

This chapter provided the opportunity to consider how far you have come in your journey. Using self-awareness, you described how you have changed. Applying self-compassion, you considered how to respond to ongoing challenges while following your heart's desire. Ultimately, making a YOU Turn was described as an ongoing process where you constantly shed light on your beliefs and change how you show up while responding to insights discovered along the way.

Accordingly, self-acceptance, the desire to see yourself clearly with all your strengths and limitations, is introduced as the final ingredient. It provides the power and motivation to continue an in-depth exploration into finding and loving yourself. Although this is the final step, there is one more aspect of your journey to consider.

So far, making a YOU Turn has been presented as a solo journey. However, you rarely travel completely alone. The quality of your encounters and your conversations with others are a significant feature of your journey. The following, and final, chapter clarifies how interactions with *fellow travelers* will amplify your journey.

Insights and Questions

Use this space to capture anything that may have surprised you
as you completed Chapter 7 or
something you may be wondering about as you continue your journey.

Key Concepts

Bypass
An experience that is used to avoid difficulties by providing temporary pleasure.

Threshold Moment
The occurrence when a previously held a belief or assumption becomes transformed into a new way of understanding. This transformation paves the way for new ways of responding.

Self-Acceptance
Embracing yourself fully for who you are including your abilities and limitations. It is a process that involves consciously approaching what matters to you by embracing the present moment as you move towards what you care about.

References

Jeffcoat T and Hayes SC. (2013). Psychologically flexible self-acceptance. In. M.E. Barnard (ed.), *The Strength of Self-Acceptance: Theory, Practice and Research*. Springer Science+Business Media, From: https://books.scholarsportal.info/uri/ebooks/ebooks3 Accessed on: 2024-08-13.

Kelly L. A Self Led Life. An On-line Training. Available: lochkelly.org/wp-content/uploads/Presentation-on-Self-Loch-Kelly-Online-Training.pdf. Accessed on: 2024-07-06.

Meyer JHF and Land R (eds).(2006). Overcoming Barriers to Student Learning: Threshold Concepts and Troublesome Knowledge. New York, NY: Routledge Publishers.

Plett, H. (2020). The Art of Holding Space. A Practice of Love, Liberation, and Leadership. Canada: Page Two Books.

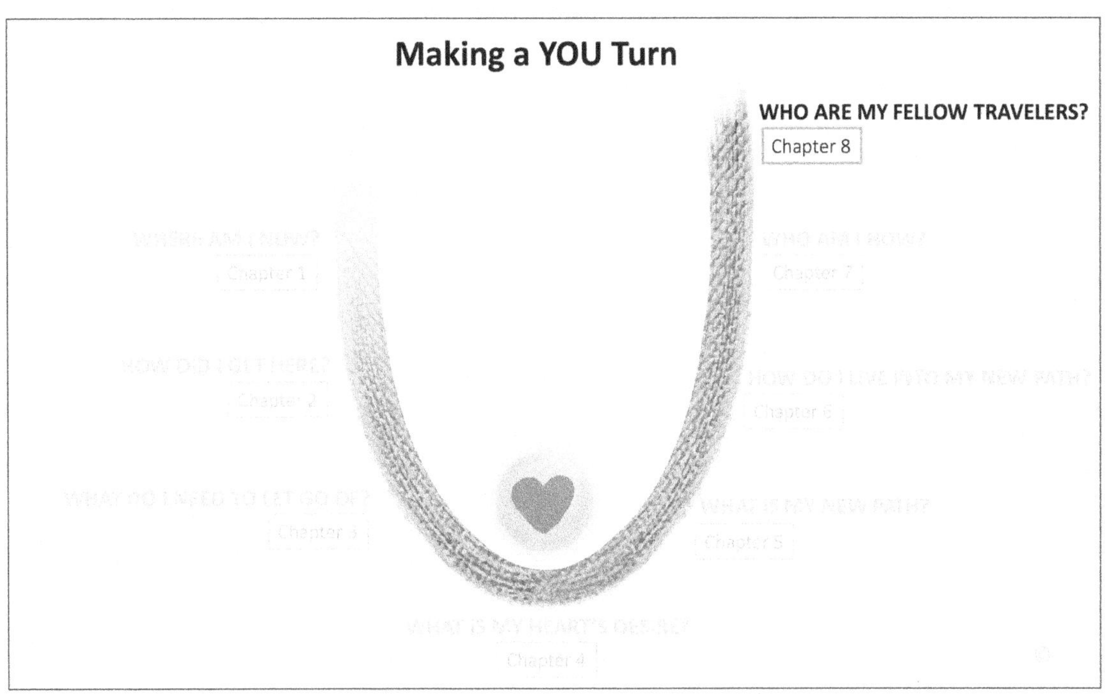

Chapter 8

Who Are My Fellow Travelers?

Welcoming Others Into Your Journey

Making a YOU Tun is not a solo journey. Odds are that as you undertake each guidepost, you will interact with others in some capacity. The purpose of this chapter is to provide guidance for navigating these relationships during your self-exploration.

For example, by virtue of your circumstances, you may naturally be in relation with others. You may be a mother, father, partner, relative, co-worker, or friend. Your fellow travelers may or may not understand or support your desire for transformation. This chapter describes how to stay on your path while sensitively steering through these relationships.

Alternatively, you may wish to deliberately engage with a group of fellow travelers—those also facing a crossroads and desire to undertake a YOU Turn. This chapter discusses how to successfully travel together on the path to finding and loving yourself.

My Invitation to You

The story below describes values held by a group of fellow travelers that I found to be particularly instrumental in supporting my journey.

As you read my story, reflect on:

- The list of values described by my Sisterhood. Are there any values that resonate most strongly with you? Are there any values that you would add?

- Do you prefer to undertake your journey with a group of fellow travelers, or do you prefer to work through this workbook on your own? Describe your preference and why.
  Remember that there is no right or wrong answer to this question!
  It is important to trust what works best for you.

The Importance of Sisterhood:
Learning to Travel with Others

It is the beginning of June 2024. I am getting ready to welcome my sisterhood into my home for our annual retreat. Our participation in the 2019 Remarkable Women's Journey created a strong bond and a desire to continue supporting each other. We have amazingly deepened our relationships through monthly virtual meetings. Our yearly in-person retreats allow us to strengthen our connection even further.

As I prepare to receive my sisters, I keep close by a summary of our responses to the question, What do you value most about our sisterhood? Superimposed words upon a picture of our overlapping hands speak clearly to what we treasure most about our journey together.

What We Value Most About Our Sisterhood
March 2020

Our Sisterhood is . . .
An unbreakable bond we hold because each and every one of us was brave enough to show up and fully participate in a unique experience. That is the secret solidarity of our sisterhood.

It is a sisterhood that makes us feel . . .

- **Deeply Accepted**
  "I can show up exactly as I am, be fully vulnerable, and know that I will be accepted without judgement"
- **Fully Supported**
  "The details of what we do don't matter. We get that everyone is fully connected in spirit"
- **Sublimely Inspired**
  "You are teachers through your wisdom, your stand and by modeling how to show up in the world in an authentic way"
- **Clearly Seen**
  "At times you see me much better than I see myself and because you see me, I can see myself. I no longer feel invisible"

Our Sisterhood allows us to . . .
Draw a collective breath as we receive the gift of joyful freedom so that we may constantly evolve into something more magnificent than we could ever have imagined on our own.

Slowly I recite the words—Accepted—Supported—Inspired—Seen. It strikes me that, put together, they spell AS IS. How appropriate. What I value most about our sisterhood are the times when we can openly share our deepest struggles in service of our ongoing journey of personal growth. As I continue to prepare for our retreat, one question guides me:

How can I create an experience that continues to deepen our trust and intimacy?

Lessons Learned

Putting into practice the well-known adage, *How do I know what I think until I hear what I say*, perhaps you would like to advance your journey by deliberately creating a group of fellow travelers so you can engage in meaningful conversations to help advance your journey. Alternatively, you may already have an established relationship with a trusted person or group and would like to further deepen these connections by traveling together. Finally, you may prefer to travel on your own.

Given that you naturally interact with others through your daily activities, whichever way you choose to travel, this guidepost will enhance your capacity for trust and intimacy when in relationships with others. Accordingly, the four guideposts for Chapter 8 are:

1. Exploring your circle of trust;
2. Asking open questions;
3. Learning to pause together;
4. Moving forward through silence.

It is important to note that since there are different ways to travel, I deliberately do not provide a specific step-by-step guide on establishing and facilitating a group of fellow travelers. Instead, this chapter focuses on the general qualities that foster trust and intimacy as you interact with others on your journey. If you desire more detailed guidance in traveling together as a group, the references provided at the end provide excellent direction.

Refresher:
Revisiting the Power of the Pause

In Chapter 6, Guidepost 2, you learned how to pause.
During the pause, you assessed your state as being either:

- Calm;
- Mobilized—ready for fight or flight or;
- Immobilized—ready to withdraw or shut down.

Take a moment to pause, assess, and revisit your experience.
What did you identify as your preferred or default state?

In this chapter, you will learn that the capacity to pause and assess your state is
particularly important when interacting with fellow travelers.

Guidepost 1: Exploring Your Circle of Trust

A circle of trust contains people with whom you can be completely vulnerable (Palmer, 2004; Plett, 2020). It can refer to a formal group that meets regularly or individuals with whom you interact. These individuals hold space for you to be open and share the most intimate details of your life without feeling any judgement or control.

You know that someone is part of your inner circle of trust when:

- You feel safe in their presence;
- They are at a similar stage of growth as you;
- You share a common language around mental health;
- You help each other to unravel old patterns and:
- You encourage each other's growth.

Ultimately, interactions with someone in your circle of trust leave you feeling refreshed and energized.

Not surprisingly, a diagram of circles is frequently used to capture different qualities associated with a circle of trust. As illustrated below, differing levels intimacy and trust offer one way of identifying who is directly within your circle of trust.

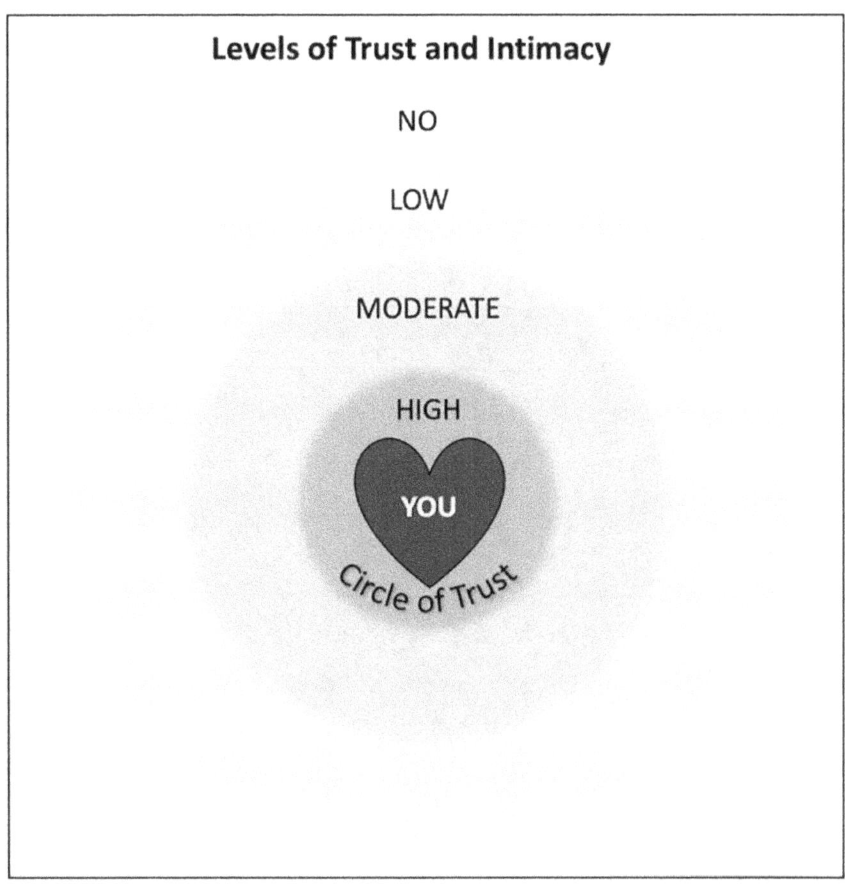

For example, some people fall into the category of *no intimacy and trust*. You may have experienced these individuals consistently breaking your trust, so it is too risky to share anything intimate. Alternatively, they may be strangers such as a ticket operator or car mechanic, so your interactions do not necessarily require any personal connection.

Relationships with more casual acquaintances are described as having *low intimacy and trust*. You may share common experiences but do not necessarily feel a personal connection. Perhaps these individuals have proven themselves to be untrustworthy in the past, or you have not had a chance to interact often enough to know if they can receive and hold your trust.

Some relationships demonstrate a *moderate state of intimacy and trust*. You might have a heart-to-heart connection with these individuals, sharing stories but find it necessary to withhold more intimate details. Often these individuals do not have the capacity to hold space for you. Instead, they may project their experiences on to you, making it difficult for you to feel safe and clearly seen. It is important to note that this more moderate state of intimacy and trust is not a reflection on you or the other person, but the result of entering the conversation with different life experiences and expectations.

Finally, there are individuals you trust with the most intimate details of your journey. These individuals may be longstanding relationships or people you have met more recently. The common factor is that you can share your story without worry of judgement and with full confidence that what you share will be held with utmost confidentiality. It is this *high level of intimacy and trust* that determines who you invite, either formally or informally, into your Circle of Trust.

Now it's Your Turn

As you undertake your journey you will not need access to a formally established circle of trust. However, it is essential to be deliberate about who falls within your circle since it can be detrimental to be open with individuals who may not understand or support your journey. This exercise helps you to identify who might consider as trustworthy and include in your circle of trust.

Exploring Your Circle of Trust

People in your circle of trust are not necessarily those with whom you spend the most time. Sometimes, your closest relationships carry expectations that make it difficult for someone to be entirely in your corner. Instead, your circle of trust contains individuals who are fully supportive, understanding, and non-judgmental of your desire for change.

YOUR CIRCLE OF TRUST

Use this space to identify individuals who you consider to be clearly in your circle of trust. Individuals with whom you can share your story without worry of judgement and with full confidence that what you share will be held with utmost confidentiality.

Guidepost 2: Asking Open Questions

In Guidepost 1, you identified individuals within your circle of trust. These are people you can count on to treat the most intimate details of your journey with great care. Your conversations with them tend to have a particular quality that allows a deeper exploration of your experiences and journey. This is mainly due to the use of open questions—the type of question that encourages you to expand on and learn more from your experience. In Guidepost 2, you consider how to ask and respond to open questions.

To begin, here is some background information that puts the importance of asking open questions into perspective.

High-trust relationships follow one simple rule: there is *no fixing, no advising, no setting each other straight* (Palmer, 2004, p. 114). Instead, the main intention of the interaction is to help you access and hear your own Inner Wisdom. This requires a particular approach to both *speaking and listening*.

The purpose of *speaking* is to give words to the truth within. You are not intending to influence the listener, to share your expertise and knowledge, or to tell a story, but rather, wanting to give a voice to your Inner Wisdom. When you are confident that you are expressing your heart's desire and feel at peace as you speak, you know your Inner Wisdom is present, and you are speaking your truth.

The purpose of *listening* is only to be present, providing the space or container for the speaker's Inner Wisdom to emerge. This means responding without commentary, judgments, experiences, or observations but with honest, open questions.

Open questions invite the speaker to go deeper within exploring their truth. These questions are:

- Short and to the point with no preamble;
- Gently paced with periods of silence to allow the speaker time to process;
- Asked with curiosity and;
- Supportive to the speaker on their journey of seeking their heart's desire.

We often ask *close questions*. These questions:

- Have a right or wrong answer;
- Require a *yes* or *no* response;
- Satisfy our curiosity;
- Do not invite the speaker to tap more deeply into their Inner Wisdom.

In making a YOU Turn, the open questions pave the way for a meaningful journey.

Now it's Your Turn

Framing an open question is challenging and takes practice. It requires careful consideration of the situation and the content and intent of the question being asked. The following exercise is designed to help develop your skills in identifying, responding to, and crafting open questions—the type of question that creates space for your Inner Wisdom to emerge.

Asking Open Questions

As a listener, asking an effective open question requires paying close attention to what the speaker is saying thus inviting them into a deeper exploration of their experience. As a speaker, you recognize an open question when asked to expand on your experience without any external assumptions or expectations.

Example:

Closed Question: Did you feel any anger in the situation you described?

Explanation: This may seem like an open question, but it presupposes that the person felt a specific emotion – anger – and so limits the speaker's response.

Rewritten into an Open Question: How do you feel about the experience you just described?

Rewrite the following two closed questions so they become open and invite the speaker to elaborate on their response.

Closed Question #1: Have you thought about seeing a therapist?

Explanation: This is a closed question since it provides advice in the form of a question.

Rewritten into an Open Question:

Closed Question #2: In your shoes I might not have (name whatever action the speaker described). What could you have done differently?

Explanation: This question starts with a preamble and implies a judgement. Feeling judged, it will cause the speaker to shut down.

Rewritten into an Open Question:

Guidepost 3: Learning to Pause Together

How you show up physically influences the quality of your connection with your fellow travelers. For example, if your body is relaxed and you feel calm, you will take your time while speaking carefully considering your words and intent. This is an ideal state for encouraging your Inner Wisdom to emerge so your truth can be clearly expressed when you are with others.

Interestingly, it is not a one-way street. When you are in a calm state, everything about you, particularly your facial expression and the quality of your eye contact invites others in your circle of trust to relax and engage. This reciprocal relationship leads to body systems that are in tune with and attuned to each other. Although you cannot physically see these connections, you know they exist when you feel deeply safe in the presence of others, and they feel clearly seen and well-supported by you.

However, as described in Chapter 6 and in the refresher at the beginning of this chapter, two additional states are available to you. As indicated on the following chart, you can show up as *mobilized*—typically characterized as fight or flight, or *immobilized* where you are withdrawn and disconnected from those around you.

State	Behavior	Impact
Calm	<ul><li>Relaxed body posture</li><li>Open facial expression</li><li>Attentive eye contact</li><li>Steady tone of voice, evenly paced</li><li>Reflective, non-judgmental listening</li></ul>	Creates a trusting, intimate space which encourages fellow travelers to relax and actively engage with curiosity speaking from their inner wisdom.
Mobilized	<ul><li>Sitting on the edge of their seat ready to spring into action</li><li>Aggressive eye contact</li><li>Speaking quickly with few pauses</li><li>Interrupts another speaker with pointed questions</li></ul>	Introduces tension into the environment resulting in a perceived lack of trust and reduced capacity to share and/or hold intimate details in the presence of fellow travelers.
Immobilized	<ul><li>Slouching posture</li><li>Averted eye contact</li><li>Speaks slowly, softly and infrequently</li><li>Not able to connect with or attend to another speaker</li></ul>	A lack of energy is introduced into the group which may cause fellow travelers to disengage and disconnect.

As shown in the chart, both states, mobilized and immobilized, have the impact of reducing capacity for trust and intimacy. Only a calm state provides the necessary foundation for effectively engaging and deepening your circle of trust.

Now It's Your Turn

Before interacting with a fellow traveler, both of you need to pause and assess what is happening for you in the moment. You want to know if both of you can be fully present and open to what is about to unfold. If something is getting in the way, it is crucial to take the time to acknowledge what is influencing you. It is also important to determine if you can shift into a calm state or if you need to reschedule your interaction for another time. The following exercise will help you make this decision.

Learning to Pause Together

Whether you are having a one-on-one conversation or as part of a group taking this journey together, ensure you enter the interaction in a way that invites deepening trust and intimacy. Before you move into a conversation, take a moment to pause together and assess your state of being.

1. **Get comfortable.** Find a position where you can be fully relaxed yet engaged. This could be on the floor or in a chair, whatever allows you to move away from paying attention to your physical comfort so you can focus on your inner state.

2. **Notice your breathing.** Without any judgment, pay attention to the quality of your breathing. Is it slow, deep, and steady? Is it rapid, shallow, and erratic?

3. **Take a scan of your body.** Starting at your head and moving slowly to your toes, identify where you may be holding tension in your body.

4. **Identify your state.** Based on the information gathered in the above 2 & 3, ask yourself what your primary state is at this moment. Is it calm, mobilized, or immobilized?

5. **Ask yourself.** Based on this assessment, ask yourself if there is something you need to do to be fully present and engaged in this conversation.

6. **Together, decide your next steps.** Depending on what you discover during your pause together, decide if your state is conducive to deepening your connection or if you would benefit from regrouping at another time.

Guidepost 4: Moving Forward Through Silence

Putting the previous three guideposts into practice allows for the emergence of a very different quality of interaction. Unlike typical conversations where you rush to fill space with our words or questions, silence becomes more commonplace. For example, as a speaker, you may rely on silence as you explore a deeper truth or insight that needs space to form before being shared with your fellow travelers. As a listener, you may need time to frame an appropriate open question. Either way, silence is a vital vehicle for listening to and moving closer to your heart's desire.

Now it's Your Turn

In our culture, it is counterintuitive to sit together in silence. The slightest moment of silence can feel very uncomfortable. It takes practice to learn how to settle into significant periods of quiet, let alone respect these moments as opportunities to connect to your Inner Wisdom. The following exercise was designed to help you become more comfortable with the experience of silence when traveling with others.

Moving Forward Through Silence

This exercise asks you to consider what role silence plays in your current conversations and then to see what happens when you deliberately introduce silence into a conversation.

1. **Your current experience with silence**

   As you reflect your conversations over the past week, what role did silence play?
   For example, can you remember any moments of silence?
   How did these moments feel?
   How do you respond to moments of silence?
   Do you feel a desire to fill the space with words, or can you sit quietly surrounded by silence?

2. **Introducing silence into your conversations**

   During the upcoming week, deliberately introduce silence into a conversation.
   For example, at the beginning of a conversation, request a few minutes of silence to settle in before you begin talking. Or, during a conversation, ask for a few minutes of silence as you consider your response. Describe your experience. Consider how long the silence lasts before you or someone else feels the need to say something.

In Summary

As laid out in this chapter, traveling effectively together requires a deliberate approach. It is important to:

- Carefully choose fellow travelers you can trust with the most intimate details of your journey;
- Create a process that supports a meaningful conversation and
- Always be aware of how you influence each other.

Given that, simply through our daily activities, we often interact with others, these are important guideposts to be aware of whether you choose to take this journey with others or on your own.

Insights and Questions

Use this space to capture anything that may have surprised you
as you completed Chapter 8 or
something you may be wondering about as you consider inviting
Fellow Travelers to accompany you as you make your YOU Turn.

Key Concepts

Circle of Trust
A circle of trust is a generic phrase used to describe those relationships which can hold and protect with care and compassion your inner most explorations.

When used as a registered trademark, a Circle of Trust® refers to an approach developed by the Center for Courage & Renewal designed to facilitate the development of groups, typically 4-6 people, who meet specifically to help individuals focus on and create clarity with respect to understanding their deeper truth. Guidelines for the development of such groups can be found in Palmer, 2004, pgs. 207-249.

Open Question
An inquiry that invites the responder to openly explore their personal experience and respond accordingly.

Closed Question
An inquiry that contains a predetermined response causing the responder to narrow their focus to providing a right answer.

References

Palmer P. J. A. (2004). Hidden Wholeness: The Journey Towards and Undivided Life. Publishers. San Francisco, CA: Jossey-Bass.

Plett H. (2020). The Art of Holding Space: A Practice of Love, Liberation, and Leadership. Canada: Page Two Books.

ADDITIONAL REFERENCES

Bourgeault C. (2003). The Wisdom Way of Knowing. Reclaiming and Ancient Tradition to Awaken the Heart. San Francisco, CA: Jossey-Bass Publishers.

Breggin P.R. (2014). Guilt, Shame, and Anxiety. Understanding and Overcoming Negative Emotions. New York, NY: Prometheus Books.

Dana D. Anchored. How to Befriend Your Nervous System. Boulder, CO: Sounds True.

Filmer-Lorch A., Barrow C. & Gill M. (2016). The Inner Power of Stillness. A Practical Guide for Therapists and Practitioners. East Lothian, UK: Handspring Publishing Inc.

Hall S.S. (2011). Wisdom. From Philosophy to Neuroscience. New York, NY: Vintage Books.

Hamilton D.M., Wilson G.M. & Loh K.M. (2020). Compassionate Conversations. How to Speak and Listen From the Heart. Boulder, CO: Shambala Publications Inc.

Hawkins D.R. (2012). Letting Go. The Pathway of Surrender. New York, NY: Hay House Inc.

Jeffers S. (2003). Embracing Uncertainty. Breakthrough Methods for Achieving Peace of Mind When Facing the Unknown. New York, NY: St. Martin's Griffin.

Palmer P.J. (2000). Let Your Life Speak. Listening for the Voice of Vocation. San Francisco, CA: Jossey-Bass Publications.

Patten T. (2018). A New Republic of the Heart. An Ethos for Revolutionaries. Berkley, CA: North Atlantic Books.

Schwartz R.C. & Falconer R.R. (2017). Many Minds, One Self. Evidence for a Radical Shift in Paradigm. Oak Park, IL: Trailheads Publications.

Schwartz R.C. & Sweezy M. (2020). Internal Family Systems Therapy. 2nd Edition. New York, NY: Guilford Publications Inc.

Shepherd P. (2017). Radical Wholeness. The Embodied Present and the Ordinary Grace of Being. Berkley, CA: North Atlantic Books.

Wheatley M.J. (2017). Who Do We Chose to Be? Facing Reality, Claiming Leadership, Restoring Sanity. Oakland, CA: Berrett-Koehler Publishers, Inc.

Whyte D. (2012). River Flow. New & Selected Poems. Revised Edition. Langley, WA: Many Rivers Press.

Wright R. (2017). Why Buddhism is True. The Science and Philosophy of Meditation and Enlightenment. New York, NY: Simon Shuster Paperbacks.

ABOUT ELAINE VAN MELLE

Elaine has spent the last 30 years facilitating transformative change in health care and health sciences education. She is an accomplished author, speaker, and workshop facilitator. Elaine is a deeply reflective, pragmatic researcher. With a degree in Microbiology and Immunology, master's in Health Administration and a Master's and PhD in Education, Elaine is particularly skilled at helping others apply theory to achieve systems change and transformation.

When faced with a personal challenge, Elaine drew from her knowledge and skills as she undertook her own journey towards personal change and transformation. She attended numerous workshops, retreats and read widely, all the time continuously applying what she learned to her own personal development. During this time, Elaine achieved Level I training in Internal Family Systems Therapy and developed expertise in the neurobiology of self-compassion. She soon realized there was a need to provide practical examples of what it looks and feels like to embrace new ways of showing up in the world. The end result is this workbook.

Through this workbook and in her presence, what people experience is Elaine's capacity to create the conditions that allow people to tap into their own inner wisdom and heart's desire. She strongly believes this inner work is the critical foundation for surviving and thriving the turbulence of our times and invites you to embark on a YOU Turn of self-discovery and transformation.

elainevanmelle.com